Visit our How To website at www.howto.co.uk

At www.howto.co.uk you can engage in conversation with our authors – all of whom have 'been there and done that' in their specialist fields. You can get access to special offers and additional content but most importantly you will be able to engage with, and become a part of, a wide and growing community of people just like yourself.

At www.howto.co.uk you'll be able to talk and share tips with people who have similar interests and are facing similar challenges in their lives. People who, just like you, have the desire to change their lives for the better – be it through moving to a new country, starting a new business, growing their own vegetables, or writing a novel.

At www.howto.co.uk you'll find the support and encouragement you need to help make your aspirations a reality.

You can go direct to www.start-and-run-a-shop.co.uk which is part of the main How To site.

How To Books strives to present authentic, inspiring, practical information in their books. Now, when you buy a title from How To Books, you get even more than just words on a page.

START AND RUN A

SHOP

How to Open a Successful Retail Business

Deborah Penrith

howtobooks / **smallbusinessstart-ups**

Published by How To Books Ltd,
Spring Hill House, Spring Hill Road,
Begbroke, Oxford OX5 1RX, United Kingdom
Tel: (01865) 375794 Fax: (01865) 379162
info@howtobooks.co.uk
www.howtobooks.co.uk

How To Books greatly reduce the carbon footprint of their books by sourcing their typesetting and printing in the UK.

British Library Cataloguing in Publication Data.
A catalogue record for this book is available from the British Library.

ISBN 978 1 84528 369 8

Produced for How To Books by Deer Park Productions, Tavistock
Typeset by PDQ Typesetting, Newcastle-under-Lyme, Staffordshire
Printed and bound in Great Britain by Cromwell Press Group, Trowbridge, Wiltshire

NOTE: The material contained in this book is set out in good faith for general guidance and no liability can be accepted for loss or expense incurred as a result of relying in particular circumstances on statements made in the book. Laws and regulations are complex and liable to change, and readers should check the current position with the relevant authorities before making personal arrangements.

CONTENTS

ACKNOWLEDGEMENTS

Retailing is an exciting, complex and vital business sector. Hopefully, this book will guide you through the challenges you may face. My thanks must go to everyone involved in helping me put it together, especially Caroline Marshall Foster, Master Florist; Mark Brown, Association of Cycle Traders (ACT); Michael Hoare, Chief Executive, The National Association of Goldsmiths (NAG); Avril McCracken, National Association of Health Stores; Sarah Holland, Flowers & Plants Association; Philippa Morrell, General Manager, BOSS Federation; Tom Algie, Owner, Practically Everything; Anian Schmitt, Only Roses in London; Amanda Hartley, Amanda's Blue Orchid Florist in Hull; Nick King, East Midlands Development Agency (emda); Steven Thain, Regional Business Link Partnership and Contract Manager, East of England Development Agency; Sophie Dimmock, London Development Agency; Mark Booker, Strategy Manager: Enterprise, Northwest Regional Development Agency; Gillian Moorhead, Senior Specialist, Business SupportTeam, One NorthEast; Rosemary Wells, Director of Business Services, South West of England Regional Development Agency; Sophie Pain, Planning Officer, Cambridge City Council; Paula Morgan, Shop and Display Equipment Association; and David and Alison Batcock, NFRN Team Design Shopfitting.

FOREWORD

A stiff breeze of change is blowing through the retail trade and this is being reflected in a more positive attitude amongst go-ahead entrepreneurs planning to open a new shop. Make no mistake, running your own business is extremely hard work, often with gruellingly long hours, but the result can be a successful retail shop that is a joy to behold. If you have a good idea and you marry it to the right business plan, your business cannot but survive, grow and flourish.

There is no doubt that a bleak economic outlook can affect the fortunes of any business. Nevertheless, you can often turn hard times to your advantage. Days of doom and gloom can be a positive spur for small businesses and offer up many new opportunities. For instance, you are more likely to react to changing market conditions by seeing gaps in the market one day and making profitable changes the next. Local shops play a vital role at the heart of communities across the nation, with research showing that the majority of consumers want access to a local shop within five minutes' walk of their home.

Define your business idea and take the steps laid out in this book to launch your new business – be inspirational, bold and single-minded. While every effort has been made to make this book as up to date as possible, things constantly change in the retail world. It is vital that you seek professional advice on all financial and legal issues. There are too many retail sectors to explore individually, but I have given explanatory insights into six diverse categories as typical examples. Remember, ideas that work for one shop may not necessarily work for another. At the end of the day, people love to shop and if you get the basic essentials right you will be well on your way to running a successful business.

As retailing guru and Topshop owner Sir Philip Green said recently, 'Retailers need to find a reason for customers to shop with you, be it service, price or style. Find a niche. Today, more than ever it's about great merchandise. You can't kid the consumer; you've got to deliver a great product.'

1
RETAILING IN THE UK

Shopkeeping through the ages

History tells us that Britain has always been regarded as a nation of shopkeepers. According to *Europe 1450 to 1789: Encyclopedia of the Early Modern World*,[1] '[i]n the late 17th . . . century there were about 40,000 shopkeepers in England and Wales'. Today, this figure has risen close to a staggering 200,000. In the ancient world trade flourished simply because some folk had a surplus of one item and coveted other goods they did not have or could not produce. The Cretans and Phoenicians of the Mediterranean were among the earliest traders and they influenced other later and greater trading civilizations. The Romans followed, establishing a sophisticated form of retailing. Archaeological digs and ruins have indicated that, amazingly, the world's first department store was in ancient Rome.

After the fall of the Roman Empire, pedlars hawked their wares by carrying their stores on their backs. They travelled from village to village selling their goods but quite often passed off inferior goods to the gullible. The streets of London rang with the cries of women selling oysters, rabbits, gingerbread, apples, watercress and dozens of other offerings. In the 12th century, tradesmen and artisans organised themselves into guilds and opened small shops. Until then, permanent buildings were quite rare. By the 13th century, fairs and markets flourished. Many had a religious foundation where people gathered at their churches on feast days and exchanged goods.

The origins of shopkeeping are lost in the mists of time. According to Dewald's authoritative *Encyclopedia*, the first shopkeepers to sell from permanent structures competed with markets and fairs selling their merchandise from the windows of their workshops between market and fair days. Shops tended to cluster in particular neighbourhoods, leaving traces in the architecture and in such street names as Fish Lane, Baker Street and Tanners Alley.

TRADING THEIR WARES

The *Encyclopedia* notes that there was a growth in tension that stoked 'conflict in [most] towns and cities in the Middle Ages, as well as in the early modern period . . . between shops and marketplaces on the one hand, and between specialised and non-specialised shops on the other . . . [They] offered a variety of goods to a variety of customers. Some sold necessities of limited value, catering to the needs of a poorer clientele. It is thought that the well-to-do of medieval cities visited local markets to purchase from foreign merchants, who could

---

[1] Dewald, Jonathan (ed.) © Gale, a part of Cengage Learning, Inc.

supply higher-quality goods in larger quantities over longer periods of time. Some shopkeepers, however, imported wares of various sorts: spices, wax, metalwares, [pottery] and silks. Their shops tended to be general stores that offered luxury commodities to wealthier patrons... [These shops were] more profitable than their common counterparts, trading in daily or popular items.'

DEVELOPING ECONOMIES

In the late 15th century and early 16th century, there was a move towards specialisation in certain forms of merchandise, but most of the early modern shopkeepers were happy to sell whatever they could. Dewald's *Encyclopedia* points out that shops and shopkeeping expanded significantly during this period as economies developed with an increase in production, distribution and consumption of goods that led to the retail revolution of early modern Europe. It was not difficult to set up in business as a shopkeeper. Wholesalers were usually willing to supply credit and this brought about a multiplication in shops. By 1789, there were more than 141,000 retail outlets in Britain. All except 21,600 were established in London.

AN EXPANDING MARKET

Throughout the 1800s, and even up until a few decades ago, food shopping for many people in the UK was a daily chore involving trips to the butcher, the fishmonger, the baker and the grocer. In the 19th century, department stores developed. Shopkeepers diversified from their main trade into other areas, which they thought would prove to be profitable. At the end of the century, one street in London would consist of a confectioner, grocer, tobacconist, pub, dairyman, tripe seller and cheesemonger.

For most of the 1800s and until the 1950s, shop assistants would serve individual customers directly. The idea of customers helping themselves was unheard of. The self-service approach where everything is on display for consumers to choose their own goods is relatively new to shopkeeping. Customers used to go in and ask to see a certain item and the assistant would get out examples from the wooden drawers and boxes behind the counter. Many ingredients, such as sugar, butter and flour, had to be weighed and bagged individually by the shop assistant before being sold to the customer. Butter was sent from the farms in barrels and whole cheeses came wrapped in muslin. Produce needed on a daily basis, such as bread, milk, fish, fruit and vegetables, was often delivered to customers' homes by horse and cart, a boy on a bike, or by van.

Until the early 19th century most people could not read so there was no point in displaying written notices over shops. Instead, metal or wood objects were hung above doorways indicating the type of merchandise sold in each particular store. Slowly, as literacy became more widespread, shops began to invest in written signs and advertisements were placed in newspapers, trade directories, and on bill boards. Logos appeared on shops and delivery vans, on carrier bags, leaflets and sale notices as part of the drive to create high profile businesses. Many merchants produced catalogues showing the range of goods they had to offer and over the years many different ways of advertising shops developed and spread.

THE RISE OF THE SUPERMARKET

In the 1920s, chain stores began to spread across the UK. Once a shop proved successful, the owner would open another branch nearby. Growing success saw the opening of branches all over the country. The first supermarket opened in the United States in 1937, laying the foundations for a revolution in shopping. Customers entered the store through turnstiles and walked through a narrow maze of shelves containing groceries. They selected their goods as they continued through the maze to a cashier. Instantly, brands and packaging became important to companies and consumers. By 1956, there were 3,000 self-service stores in operation in the UK and as these shops grew in size they became known as supermarkets.

For the modern supermarket customer the experience of shopping is not comparable with shopping in the past. Rather than shopping everyday from a selection of specialist shops, supermarket customers tend to visit the store, often by car, and stock up with a week's worth of supplies in one go. Today, 75% of Britain's total grocery market is controlled by its four largest supermarkets.

SHOPPING IN THE FUTURE

In years to come, visits to a supermarket may become a thing of the past. Today, there is the added advantage of food consumers being able to shop online in virtual stores and arrange delivery to their homes. However, interest in food miles, the growth of farmer's markets and organic delivery schemes shows that some customers avoid buying food from supermarkets altogether.

For many consumers, modern food retailing and particularly the supermarket is a sign of progress that saves consumers time and money and offers exceptional choice. For others, the supermarket groups are blamed for the disappearance of smaller grocery shops, the increase in the use of motor cars, and suggestions that unfair dealings often target farmers and food manufacturers.

Definition of 'retail'
Middle English, from Anglo-Norman, variant of Old French; *retaille*, piece cut off, from *retaillier*, to cut.

Today's world

One tenth of the UK population works in the retail sector in a range of diverse businesses, from large chains to small individual shops. According to the British Retail Consortium (BRC), 9% of all VAT-registered businesses in the UK are retailers, with the total number currently at 197,990. Retail is the largest sector employer in the UK with 3 million employees (11% of the total UK workforce). The sector's sales are worth £278 billion, a third of consumer spending, generating almost 8% of the gross domestic product in the UK.

Around half a million people take the plunge and start up their own business each year and there are more than 4.3 million small businesses in the UK. Of these, 2.72 million are sole proprietors. Small and medium-sized enterprises (SMEs) employ 12 million people, 58% of the private sector workforce, and turnover totals £1.2 billion, some 50% of the UK gross domestic product.

The number of start-up businesses is increasing. There are always opportunities, even in more challenging times, and really there is no such thing as a good time or bad time to start a small business. If you consider certain basic factors and you follow good practice, any time can be the right time to start up. The golden rule of the right item, at the right time, in the right place, at the right price is the foundation of good retailing.

Before starting up, some factors to consider include the following.
□ There is scope for niche enterprises, but you must meet and deliver what is needed.
□ Selling capability is a priority and knowing exactly how you are going to sell to your market is a must.
□ Research everything you need to know about the sector you're entering, including your competitors, whether your prices are right, whether you're compliant with all regulations, and have uncovered all the hidden costs involved in starting up.
□ You will need sufficient start-up and ongoing working capital in place to get you up and running and make sure the repayments don't choke you within the first six months.
□ Run a market test to confirm that your target market is willing to pay for your intended product or service.
□ Focus on offering quality, both in goods and service.
□ Make sure you are good at and enjoy your chosen field so that you end up excelling at it.

The UK is currently listed as the sixth easiest country in the world in which to do business. Yet many still complain that the volume of regulation is too high, too complex and presents too many conflicting demands. The Department for Business, Innovation and Skills (BIS, www.bis.gov.uk) broadly rates the following as obstacles to business success:

□ competition in the market 15%;
□ regulations 14%;
□ taxation, VAT, PAYE, National Insurance, business rates 12%;
□ the economy 10%;
□ cash flow 10%;
□ recruiting 6%;
□ shortage of skills generally 4%;
□ availability/cost of suitable premises 4%;
□ obtaining finance 3%;

☐ no obstacles 2%;
☐ shortage of managerial skills/expertise 1%.

It is interesting to note that, contrary to what you might expect, raising the necessary cash is far from being the major obstacle you will face. That role is reserved for competition in the marketplace.

The government launched the Enterprise Strategy in March 2008, with the aim of making the UK the most enterprising economy in the world and the best place to start and grow a business. It is designed to unlock the nation's entrepreneurial talents, boost enterprise skills and knowledge, help new and existing businesses to get funding to start up and grow, and ease the burden of regulation – particularly on small firms which feel its impacts most. The strategy sets out five key enablers as listed below.

☐ A culture of enterprise – where everyone with entrepreneurial talent is inspired and not afraid to take up the challenge of turning ideas into wealth.
☐ Knowledge and skills – equipping employees and owners with the tools to unlock their entrepreneurial talent.
☐ Access to finance – ensuring that entrepreneurs and small business owners have the knowledge, skills and opportunity to access the finance they need to make their enterprising ideas a reality.
☐ Regulatory framework – keeping legislation to a minimum, reducing the burdens of regulation, inspection and enforcement, without removing essential protections, and clearly communicating any changes.
☐ Business innovation – ensuring that UK businesses are in a position to capitalise on global trends, by helping them to develop and successfully commercialise innovative products, process and services.

For more information on how this strategy may help you, contact BIS.

Familiarising yourself with retail terminology

Barcode
A series of vertical or horizontal parallel lines forming a code that is read using photoelectric devices and software and interpreted by a barcode scanner.

Chargebacks
The retailer's invoice for claims against a supplier resulting from items such as damaged goods, adjustments and the recovery of transportation charges for improperly routed merchandise.

Consumer sentiment
Consumer sentiment is a measurement of consumers' attitudes regarding their own financial situation, and their feelings about the overall economy in the present and the future.

Cost complement
The average relationship existing between the cost of merchandise and the retail value of the items handled during an accounting period.

Customer loyalty programme
A structured, long-term marketing exercise that provides incentives to repeat customers who demonstrate loyalty in buying goods.

Layaway
A method of deferring payments where goods are kept by the store until the customer has completed payments for them.

Markdown
A reduction of an original or previous retail price.

Mark-up
The difference between the cost price of goods and their retail price. Also referred to as mark-on or gross margin.

Mark-up cancellations
A reduction in the price of an item after it has been subject to an additional mark-up.

Markdown cancellations
The increase in the retail price of an item that has been reduced.

Merchandising
A practice that contributes to the sale of products to a retail consumer.

Promotional markdowns
A lowering of the retail price hoping to encourage greater store traffic.

Retail price
The price at which goods are offered for sale.

Shrinkage
The gradual loss of stock over time due to damage, misplacement or theft.

Speciality stores
Retail outlets that maintain a large selection in a limited line of merchandise.

Stock book
A book where additions to stock are entered in the form of goods received from suppliers and merchandise deductions, which represent sales to customers.

Trade discount
A deduction from the agreed price to encourage prompt payment of bills.

Universal Product Code (UPC)
A categorisation where each item is given a ten-digit number, pre-marked on the package in the form of a barcode over ten corresponding numbers.

Visual merchandising
The display of products that makes them appealing, attractive, accessible, engaging and enticing to shoppers in a retail store. Visual merchandising uses colour, lighting, displays, smells, sounds, digital technology and interactive elements to catch customers' attention and persuade them to make purchases.

Advantages of being an olderpreneur

Older people bring their whole life experience to a business. Companies started by older people have a 70% chance of surviving the crucial first five years, compared to 28% for those started by younger people, according to Hilary Farnworth of the London Metropolitan University. Senior entrepreneurs contribute £24.4 billion to the UK economy. There is a massive saving to the public purse. It costs £7,000 a year to keep someone aged over 50 on benefits.

Laurie South, Chief Executive of the Prince's Initiative for Mature Enterprise (PRIME), says:

Many older people are better placed to go into business than their younger counterparts. Older people have better personal skills and usually have an established support network around them. They may have fewer problems with work-life balance; their children have grown up, and there's less pressure to perform. They are more likely to be realistic and understand that there is a lot of luck involved in running a successful business. But the desire to succeed must still be strong.

According to Professor David Storey of Warwick Business School:

The number of olderpreneurs has been rising. Thirty years ago the majority of self-employed were in the 30–44 age range. In 1977, 11% of men aged 45–64 were self-employed, compared with 13% of those aged 30–44; by 2000 it was 15% of the 45–64 group, but still 13% of the younger age range. The two groups are likely to have different motivations. Those in their twenties or thirties are likely to be generating money for themselves and their families, and will go through intense pain and hardship if they think they are going to strike it big in a few years.

The time horizon of someone in their late fifties is very different. They need more instant gratification. If you are going to grow a business substantially there are two necessary conditions: a strong motivational element and a strong element of luck. It's clear that businesses run by more mature people have higher survival rates but lower growth rates. In a time of huge economic uncertainty, many olderpreneurs may be forced into self-employment by dwindling pensions or age discrimination in the job market.

The chance of finding employment if you are made redundant over the age of 45 is only one in ten, according to research from PRIME. Self-employment may be the only option. You may not make millions but you can earn a living or top up an inadequate pension.

2
GETTING STARTED

Starting your own business is an exciting time and, with a little bit of research and a lot of passion and hard work, you can make it a reality. Think about what you'd love to do, what you are good at, what you are passionate about. You've got to have a great idea that is sustainable in a competitive environment. You must distinguish your chosen shop as a niche operation that fills a void of some kind.

Considering your personal strengths and weaknesses

However, it's not enough just to have a viable idea. Owning your own shop consumes your time and energy and is demanding of effort. You will also need to have the right skills and temperament to make it a success. Entrepreneurs in the UK clock up 50-hour working weeks, so it is not a part-time commitment or hobby. It is vital you know yourself. Self-evaluation, identifying your needs and understanding your personality type will help you make the correct choices. Appraise your strengths and weaknesses honestly.

Start by asking yourself these searching questions.

- ☐ Could you run your own business?
- ☐ Do you have self-confidence and bundles of enthusiasm?
- ☐ Do you get on with people and enjoy talking to them?
- ☐ Are you curious about strangers?
- ☐ Are you outgoing?
- ☐ Are you self-disciplined?
- ☐ Are you ready to put in the long hours of working a retail week?
- ☐ Can you make careful decisions?
- ☐ Can you cope under stress?
- ☐ Do you have the determination when the going gets tough?
- ☐ Can you learn from your mistakes and take advice?
- ☐ Are you tolerant enough to handle complaining or difficult customers?
- ☐ Are you well organised and responsible?

The key is to develop and grow your own skills and characteristics as you gain more experience. You will also need support from your family, so involve them right from the beginning and keep them up to date on how things are moving along. You can also use them as a sounding board and to provide feedback. You may also wish to get a good mentor on board as two heads are always better than one.

Alarm Bell

When you run your own business it is your life. There is no such thing as nine to five. Only employees can go home and forget about work. You will live and breathe the job.

Having spoken to many business owners and entrepreneurs, the following personal characteristics have always emerged at the forefront:

- □ motivated;
- □ driven and enthusiastic;
- □ organised;
- □ professional;
- □ hard-working – self-discipline and commitment;
- □ perseverant – persistence and stickability;
- □ patient – giving it time to work;
- □ pro-active in finding customers;
- □ self-confident;
- □ communication skills – verbal and non-verbal;
- □ selling skills;
- □ customer care – going the extra mile, keeping in touch;
- □ literate and numerate;
- □ honest;
- □ setting realistic goals and objectives;
- □ networking;
- □ computer literate;
- □ time-keeping – reliability;
- □ competitive;
- □ willing to make sacrifices – time;
- □ decisive;
- □ looking out for opportunities;
- □ open minded;
- □ willing to learn;
- □ sense of humour;
- □ assertive;
- □ working alone – no one to bounce ideas off;
- □ coping with routine and monotony;
- □ having family support.

Developing a business sense

The association or professional body relevant to your projected business will be able to tell what formal standards or qualifications are required for your shop category. The Directory of British Associations should be available at your local city or central library. Alternatively try the Trade Association Forum (www.taforum.org) for further information.

Business skills are essential if you do not already have them. It is important to understand the principles of business and management including marketing, strategic planning, accounts, personnel management and so on. Ideally, aim to get some basic training in business administration before you start.

If you have no general business experience, it may be worth taking a business start-up or management course. Often these are available locally and may be free of charge or of minimal cost. Contact your local Business Link or adult education college for details of courses available in your area. learndirect (www.learndirect.co.uk) also provides courses for new start-ups. Opening a shop also requires an element of selling and it is possible to learn basic selling techniques.

In addition, mathematics is used at every level of retailing, from the basic functions of counting money, calculating gross profit margins, cash flow, start-up costs, break-even analysis and profitability, to computing the total amount of a sales transaction involving the calculation of percentages to determine discounts and VAT. So it's important to brush up on your numeracy skills.

RETAIL COURSES

Typically, retail management degrees include a combination of business modules such as human resource management, marketing, finance and IT, together with in-depth study of retail functions, such as buying and merchandising, store operations, supply chain management and the retail environment. The advantage is that you will be prepared for the world of business, with a focus on retail. Each college or university has a different approach and emphasis to these courses.

Retail has long been considered a sector that lacks the full range of skills and qualifications needed in a customer-focused industry, according to the National Skills Academy (NSA) for Retail. A quarter of employees lack the equivalent of a Level 2 NVQ, while 40% of sales staff do not have five good GCSEs. Fifteen in every hundred have no qualifications whatsoever.

Skills Shops (www.skillsmartretail.com)

However, Skillsmart Retail's vision is to establish the NSA for Retail as the definitive answer to the skills needs of retailers, employees and those hoping to work in retail. The NSA for Retail will be run through a network of local high street retail Skills Shops, offering training and support to everyone from pre-employment through to degree level. Taking the form of one-stop, walk-in or virtual Skills Shops on high streets and in shopping centres across the UK, each will be run individually by local stakeholders, including developers, training providers, Jobcentre Plus and retailers.

This network will provide access to world-class skills and business support for retailers whatever their size, wherever they are located. It will also create a consistent national approach for training and skills in the UK's largest private industry sector. Forty new sites will be united with 30 existing independent Skills Shops currently operating in key locations. These include Manchester Arndale, The Source at Meadowhall in Sheffield, Twickenham's Hawk Training, Touchwood Centre in Solihull, King's Lynn, Derby's Workstation, Cabot's Circus Skills Shop in Bristol, Lakeside, Heathrow and Bluewater. Each Skills Shop will be tailored to meet specific local requirements, as well as the needs of individuals.

International Correspondence School (ICS) (www.icslearn.co.uk)
BTEC in Retail Management – Level 2
Introduces how different retailers operate within a specified territory, the IT systems they adopt, and how legislation affects the retail operation. Master the basics, including techniques to merchandise, display and promote products most effectively to increase sales. Understand the different distribution channels, and stock control and security systems used in retail. You'll also develop skills in managing customer services as well as staff. Suitable if you are already working in the retail sector and wanting to gain an industry recognised qualification, or whether you are thinking of changing careers to work in retail.

learndirect (www.learndirect.co.uk)
Offers retail training for staff through its Retail Skills NVQ – Level 2, which combines work-based competency assessment with online courses that can be tailored to your own business needs. This can be ideal for expanding your staff's understanding of retail operations and principles.

Universities offering retail studies
A number of universities offer retail qualifications in Retail Management, Retail Marketing, Fashion and Textile Retailing and Business Studies (Retailing). These include:

- University of Bedfordshire (www.beds.ac.uk);
- University of Brighton (www.brighton.ac.uk);
- Buckinghamshire New University (www.bucks.ac.uk);
- University of Wales Institute, Cardiff (www.uwic.ac.uk);
- University of Central Lancashire (www.uclan.ac.uk);
- The Manchester College (www.ccm.ac.uk);
- The University of Kent (www.kent.ac.uk);
- Leeds Metropolitan University (www.leedsmet.ac.uk);
- London Metropolitan (www.londonmet.ac.uk);
- The University of Manchester (www.manchester.ac.uk);
- The Manchester Metropolitan University (www.mmu.ac.uk);
- University of Northampton (www.northampton.ac.uk);
- Queen Margaret University, Edinburgh (www.qmu.ac.uk);
- Roehampton University, London (www.roehampton.ac.uk);
- University of Westminster, London (www.westminster.ac.uk).

Researching your market

Find out as much as you can about your market and then look for a gap you can fill. Identify if there is a market for your business, what demand there will be for your products, who will buy your products and who your competitors are. This will build up a picture for your retail business. Focus on current trends: is the market expanding or declining, and what is the forecast for the next couple of years?

Check the demographics of your area to get a general idea of your potential customers. What age and economic bracket are you aiming for? Study the foot traffic past your business. Are there cafes, restaurants, hotels or a post office nearby where people may stop and browse in your shop?

This sort of quantitative research produces numerical data which can be used to determine the size of your market, how much it is worth, where the specific growth areas lie, and trends in the retail sector. It can also provide details of who your customers will be, their age, gender, marital status, occupation, income, lifestyle and location. Qualitative research helps you to understand the attitude and beliefs of your customers.

 To be successful, you need to stand out from the rest, especially on entering a highly competitive market. A unique selling proposition (USP) provides a clear reason why customers should buy from you rather than someone else.

Try to define and consider the following.

- ☐ Who might your customers be?
- ☐ What are the age, sex, income and occupation of the people you want to attract?
- ☐ If there are changes taking place, how might they affect what you offer?
- ☐ How much demand is there for your products?
- ☐ What prices would people be prepared to pay?
- ☐ Who is the competition?
- ☐ How reliable are suppliers?

True marketing research also encompasses:

- ☐ product research;
- ☐ sales research;
- ☐ advertising research.

Effective market research should provide all the clues needed to forecast the future. This should provide key information regarding the following.

- ☐ Trends in the economy – for example, how inflation affects spending power.
- ☐ Trade trends – read articles in the trade press.

□ Competitor activity – if competitors are changing their product or tactics, take note of their methods.

□ The weather – seasonal fluctuations will affect the type of products to sell.

Says Tom Algie, owner of Practically Everything in Settle:

Before starting out, do as much research as possible in your spare time, thinking about what to sell at what price. Roughly estimate customers per day and the spend of each customer a day. Consider what the current trends are in the particular line of business you are thinking about. Look at the local competition and how good their customer service is. Think whether you are suitable, for instance do you like people? What will happen if you only sell half the volume you planned? Your core costs are key to this: low rent and rates – or a rent-free period, heating, lighting and other costs. Basically until these are all covered from your sales, you make absolutely no money at all.

RESEARCH RESOURCES

There are various forms of research sources you can use. The first place to go is your local library. If you are able to get to London, the newly opened Business and Intellectual Property Centre (BIPC) at the British Library (www.bl.uk/bipc) has huge resources available for people looking to set up their own business and it is free. The available information includes 7,000 printed market research reports covering every kind of market you can think of and giving details of the major players, the size of their market share, the sector's potential for growth and so on. The library staff can point you in the right direction for retailing. You can also book a free 30-minute advice session with a member of staff to go through in detail what you need and how to get the most out of the available resources.

If you are unable to get to London, other libraries with good business resource centres include Norfolk and Norwich Millennium Library, Manchester Central Library, Scotbis at the National Library of Scotland in Edinburgh, Belfast Central Library and Flexible Support for Business (www.flexible-support-wales.gov.uk) which has several business resource centres in Wales.

You can also do a lot of market research online, from finding out about seasonal trends and demographics to researching your competitors, by using an internet search engine. There are plenty of existing retail shops with websites. This means that small start-up businesses have as much of a chance as bigger competitors of finding the information they need. Make sure the websites you use are reliable and contain up-to-date information.

Business Link (www.businesslink.gov.uk) is another good place to start; its information service can tell you what research is available and how to get it. If you need to commission market research, Business Link advisers can help you draw up a brief and find a market researcher to do the work.

Other useful sources include the National Statistics Office (www.statistics.gov.uk), BIS (www.bis.gov.uk), and the Chamber of Commerce in your area. Some market research sites are www.freshminds.co.uk and www.snapdata.co.uk You can find information on market trends from Mintel (www.mintel.co.uk), Key Note (www.keynote.co.uk), Euromonitor (www.euromonitor.co.uk and Datamonitor (www.datamonitor.co.uk). UpMyStreet (www.upmystreet.com) provides postcode local statistics and socio-economic profiles for local areas.

For information on competitors and who may be trading in your area, try the *Yellow Pages* (www.yell.com), *Thomson Directory* (www.thomsonlocal.com), British Companies (www. britishcompanies.co.uk) and the British Chambers of Commerce (www.chamber online.co.uk).

Contact people who have a similar business to the one you are planning to open, especially if they won't be your direct competition. Most small business owners are happy to tell you about their experiences and share advice and pointers. Talk to friends and other people who might buy your products. It's also a good idea to travel to niche shops that would be similar to yours but are in another city or county to check out their merchandise, ask the owners why they chose their locations, and get information about their customer base.

SILVER V YOUNG CONSUMERS

According to Verdict Research (www.verdict.co.uk), due to increased longevity and the ageing of post-war baby boomers, the population of over-65s is set to swell over the next 20 years. The number of senior citizens in the UK will have risen 40% to 13.4 million. The growth will be strongest between 2009 and 2014 when there will be an addition of 1.3 million people to the age group.

This segment's participation in retail is currently lower than average in every sector, apart from food and grocery. For instance, older customers are generally less interested in the latest clothing fashions, homeware, design or technological advancements and they therefore shop less for these types of goods. This is not because older consumers are lacking in cash. There is a growing number of affluent over-65s who have private final salary pensions and have also made significant profits from rising house prices in the past.

By comparison, young consumers, generally aged 15 to 24, spend proportionally far less on food and groceries and place a greater emphasis on comparison shopping, particularly music, DVDs, clothing and footwear.

Legal considerations

There are a number of regulations you must comply with when starting a new business. To operate within the law, you must follow several procedures and you will also have to contact a number of government agencies. You will also have to register with your local authority and, if you employ staff, there are many regulations and employment laws to which you must adhere.

The main regulations covered within this book include:

- legal status;
- trading name of the business;
- insurance;
- employing staff;
- tax and financial issues;
- planning permission;
- licences;
- health and safety;
- fire safety;
- data protection;
- trading regulations.

The following is meant as guidance only on how to trade and name your business. You should seek professional advice before making any business decisions that may have legal implications.

Forming a business

The legal status of your business will determine which regulations are necessary. When you set up your business, you need to decide at an early stage how you intend to structure it as your status can have both legal and practical implications. There are four main business structures.

- Sole trader (self-employed).
- Partnership (self-employed people working together).
- Limited company.
- Community interest companies (CICs).

SOLE TRADER

Most people who first set out in business choose to be sole traders. This simply means you have complete control and are solely responsible for your business's profit and loss. Sole trader is the simplest, quickest and cheapest form of business to set up and has its own advantages and disadvantages that need to be carefully considered.

If you choose to be a sole trader you will be self-employed and personally liable for any debts the business incurs. As there is an unlimited liability for debts, if your business loses money you may wind up having to sell your personal assets. On the upside, you get to keep all the profits you make. Start-up formalities are minimal and costs are low.

Sole traders can employ people and are able to give a more personal service to customers. You are also able to make changes within your business very quickly.

You need to keep simple accounts and complete a self-assessment tax return to HM Revenue & Customs (HMRC, www.hmrc.gov.uk) each year, detailing your income and expenses.

You also have to keep records of all your income and expenses.

To become a sole trader, you must register as self-employed with HMRC within the first three months of starting up. If you fail to do so, you could face a penalty of £100.

Tax and National Insurance (NI) payments are likely to be lower than for a limited company structure, but sole traders are personally liable for business debts and they are entitled to fewer social security benefits. You must pay income tax on any profits your business makes in the form of National Insurance Contributions (NICs), either Class 2 or Class 4. HMRC offers local one-day courses on how to become a sole trader.

You also need to register for VAT if you expect your turnover is going to be more than £68,000 a year.

PARTNERSHIP

A partnership is a business arrangement where two or more people (up to a maximum of 20) are self-employed and in business together to make a profit. All partners share the business costs, profits and debts. Partnerships work well when each partner brings a different skill or area of expertise to the business and the workload is divided up to reflect each of the partner's strengths.

You then need to consider if an ordinary or limited partnership would be the best for your business. In an ordinary partnership the partner or partners take on unlimited liability for any debts incurred by the business and all profits are shared equally. Limited partnerships accept limited liability to the amount invested and, while profits are shared equally, the responsibility and control of the business lies with the ordinary partners. Limited partners are often seen as 'sleeping partners' as they do not directly involve themselves with the company.

While there are no legal obligations set for ordinary partners, it is recommended that a partnership agreement be arranged to legalise the partnership. This will help to avoid any disputes that may arise. It is recommended that you use a solicitor to draft this agreement, which should cover the following points.

- ☐ The amount of capital each partner will invest.
- ☐ The profit ratio dependent on the amount invested.
- ☐ Debt liabilities – whether for an ordinary or limited partnership.

If you decide that a partnership is the best way forward for your business, you should first decide how many partners could benefit the business. Then think about how you would like the partners to integrate within the company. Finally, consider the following.

- ☐ Partners' capabilities to drive the business forward.
- ☐ Leadership qualities and management experience.
- ☐ Level of specialist knowledge and expertise.
- ☐ Level of trust associated with the partners.

☐ Seniority and control over the business.
☐ The rules on admitting new partners.
☐ Rules on ending the partnership.

LIMITED COMPANY

Setting up a limited company is the most common alternative. Even though you own it and work for it, a limited company is a separate entity, which means you will only be personally liable for debts in exceptional circumstances. Compared to sole tradership, there will be more administration required by you and NI payments may be higher.

If you are starting a limited company, most people use a registration or formation agent, solicitor or accountant. A limited company must be registered with Companies House. Formation agents, such as the National Business Register, use their own software which works directly with the Companies House system. Typically costs start at about £200, depending on the level of service you require.

A key advantage to using an agent is the advice they can give you on compiling the necessary documents and the correct structure for your business. Companies House does not offer this service when registering. Alternatively, you can use an online registration company, which usually costs about £80 to £100 including fees, but this can take three to eight days.

LIMITED LIABILITY COMPANY

A limited liability company (LLC) is one whose shareholders have limited liability for the company's debts. Their liability is restricted to the value of the shares that they own or the guarantees they sign. A limited liability partnership (LLP) aims to combine the flexibility of a partnership arrangement with the benefits of limited liability. It is doubtful you will choose either of these legal structures in a retail shop set-up.

COMMUNITY INTEREST COMPANY

A community interest company (CIC) is a new type of company. Essentially it is a limited company that wants to use its profits and assets for the public good. CICs are designed for social enterprises, including local community enterprises, social firms and mutual organisations, such as co-operatives. Co-operatives are businesses that are collectively owned and controlled by the people who work for it. At least two people must be involved. For more information contact the Community Interest Companies Regulator, www.cicregulator.gov.uk

NAMING YOUR BUSINESS

Choosing a name is a long-term decision and another important part of the planning stage. Create a catchy name for your business that will portray a certain image and provide good marketing potential. While you are no longer required to register your business name with any government department, there are laws about using certain names and disclosing certain details of ownership.

If you are a sole trader, you can trade under your own name or choose a different business name. A partnership can trade under the names of all the partners or a business name. A limited company or limited liability partnership can trade under its registered name or use a different business name. If you buy an off-the-shelf company you can apply to change the registered name.

To further protect your business name from use by others you can register it as a trade mark or a domain name, or both. The Patent Office regulates trade mark registration. An agent can check for names already registered as trade marks. This usually costs from £50 to £80. To check web domain names free of charge, search at a name registration service such as www.netnames.co.uk

When you have decided on the name, you must check that there is not a business already trading under that name. You can do this through Companies House (www.companieshouse.gov.uk) or use a company registration agent.

If you do not trade under exactly the same name as appears on your stationery, shop signs or bank details, you need to let your customers know your name and the business address where you can be contacted. For example, if your name is 'S. Smith' and your business trades as 'S. Smith', you do not have to disclose these. However, if your business stationery and banking details are 'S. Smith Toys', you have to disclose.

Certain names are not allowed and they must not be misleading or likely to cause confusion with an existing business. Names judged to be offensive are also banned by Companies House. Certain words are prohibited by law, for example British, Royal and Bank. The Companies House booklet GBF2 details prohibited words.

To test your business name you could follow these parameters.
- ☐ Is it easy to pronounce and spell?
- ☐ Is it distinctive and concise?
- ☐ Does it clearly communicate your message?
- ☐ Does it have a positive sound?

Get feedback from friends and family, repeat it often and if, after a few days you feel confident and comfortable with the name, go for it! However, if you fall in love with a name that doesn't really tell people what you do or what you sell, consider adding a tagline. This is a phrase or adage that defines your company's mission in the fewest words possible.

Getting started checklist

- ☐ Your key categories.
- ☐ Assessing your shop.
- ☐ Understanding your area.
- ☐ Stocking the right product lines.
- ☐ Merchandising to maximise sales.
- ☐ Getting the right shop layout.
- ☐ Checking you have the right equipment.
- ☐ Training for you and your staff.
- ☐ Operating systems.
- ☐ Working with suppliers.

3
WALKING THE BUSINESS TIGHTROPE

The financial road to success is tough and seemingly always uphill. Each day is filled with challenges and the need to make decisions based on which course to follow. Be sure you have enough financial backing to pay bills and buy enough merchandise for at least two years. Good fiscal management is important in any economic situation but it is not always possible to have financial management skills as well as a creative mind.

If the financial side of business is foreign to you, the first thing you need to know is where to get help. Attend some basic business seminars, a business course or adult evening classes. Financial institutions and government departments, such as Business Link, are willing to give you free advice. The more financially prepared and knowledgeable you are about starting your business, the more you can count on success. Many businesses fail because they lack financial management knowledge or did not pay enough attention to this important area.

Choosing the right finance

These days, banks are far more cautious about how much they lend and to whom. They regard small businesses as 'high risk', which allows them to demand more security on loans, increase charges and apply high rates. However, there are active backers out there. Private investors are still eager to find good prospects. Informed venture capitalists, known as business angels, are a huge source of finance but you need to be creative about how you put a deal together.

Networking can help you identify the private individuals with money and will help you find out which managers at which banks are still doing deals. Also take a look at regional grants, loans and investment schemes. The maximum for small business loans has increased from £30,000 to £50,000 but you need to work hard to win. Your proposition has to demonstrate a business model that is revenue generating, with significant growth momentum, and that is well articulated.

Also look at your own personal savings and assets. If you have a redundancy payment, a maturing ISA, an inheritance, a life insurance policy, or can take out a second mortgage, you might actually have the necessary capital to fund your business yourself. Cash in the bank can be a useful source of working capital to help you during the first few months.

However, only consider securing a loan against personal assets if you want to make a long-term investment in your business. You can then factor the repayment costs into your business plan. Raising the money yourself is a good way of keeping control of your business and means you don't owe money to anyone else.

RAISING MONEY

Overdrafts

Most banks and building societies offer commercial loans but will lend you money only against some form of security. The first option is to agree to an overdraft amount that your bank will let you borrow without notice. In return, you pay interest on the sum borrowed and possibly a service or set-up charge. Interest is usually calculated on a daily basis so you pay only for what you borrow.

Overdrafts are useful for temporary financing or fluctuating cash shortages, such as seasonal fluctuations or having to pay suppliers before you receive payment from customers. They are quick and convenient to arrange and are flexible. Your overdraft should be used only to temporarily pay for day-to-day business running costs, such as bills and wages or buying stock.

Loans

If you are able to persuade the bank that you will be able to generate a steady and predictable cash flow, you may be able to take out a small, unsecured loan. However, a long-term loan may be the best way to finance your business. Many are for a fixed period of one to ten years. Loan repayments must be made monthly and will include bank finance costs. For any borrowing you will need to provide security, either a personal guarantee (assets) or a guarantee from a third party who will be liable to pay the debt if you default.

Credit cards

Credit and charge cards are a variable and convenient short-term means of borrowing cash, paying bills and making purchases, regardless of how much is in your bank account. Using these cards can reduce your bank charges because you are writing fewer cheques. They are also an expeditious and convenient method of payment and can give you up to 56 days of free credit. The itemised billing means that you can analyse your spending patterns quickly and clearly, which helps with your bookkeeping.

Some credit cards offer 0% interest on balance transfers for 9 to 15 months. You could take advantage of this by continually transferring your balance from one card to another, effectively borrowing for nothing. Look out for the annual fixed charge and remember that if you don't clear your monthly balance within the specified time, you will incur stiff charges. Credit cards should only be used as a short-term funding solution and you may find that a bank loan is a more suitable option if the borrowing is ongoing.

Although about two-thirds of all businesses go to their bank for funding, there are other common sources of money to start up your business, among them family and friends, specialist backers, and grants.

Family and friends

If you should ask family and friends, go for either a loan or an investment. If it is a loan you should agree a fixed repayment period and rate of interest. However, they may be willing to offer a low interest loan, or one with no interest attached at all. If they make an investment they will hold equity in your company in the form of profits. They will expect a percentage of the profits and the ability to sell their stake in the business at some time in the future.

It is important that any loan or investment should be underpinned with a formally drawn-up agreement explaining everyone's liabilities, obligations and expectations to avoid damaging future relationships.

Specialist backers

Venture capitalists (VCs) are professional fund management companies prepared to give potential high-fliers significant backing. They tend to have high minimum investment levels and are not usually interested in the level of funding small companies need. VCs invest money, rather than lend it, in return for shares in the business and normally look for a minimum return of between 30% and 40% a year over five years.

The process of raising venture capital will take about three to six months and these companies typically invest only in 2% to 5% of the proposals they see. Check with the British Venture Capital Association (www.bvca.co.uk) for some of the UK's principal institutions.

Business angels

A business angel is an informal venture capitalist who is willing to provide equity finance to a small business. They are private individuals, normally entrepreneurs or retired executives, who expect to receive shares in the business in return for providing cash to start up a venture. They may also be prepared to share their experience, advice and contacts to help a business really take off.

Typically, a business angel would be prepared to invest between £10,000 and £750,000. The Chambers of Commerce state that business angels are a significant source of start-up and early-stage capital for companies without a track record. A business plan based on powerful market research is essential when contacting these organisations.

Potential sources of business angels may include your bank, your local Business Link, or one of the organisations that exist to bring the two together. You can also find one through the British Business Angels Association (BBAA, www.bbaa.org.uk). Look through the online member directory and choose a business angel most suited to your needs, in terms of specialisation, investment criteria and geographic location.

The business sections of a number of newspapers also include advertisements from investors and from businesses looking for finance.

Grants

If you have no security to offer, you may be entitled to some form of grant. There is a variety of grants available to small businesses from central and local government, as well as a range of organisations and trusts (see the section following on Government Help and Support). However, many sources require you to raise half of the amount you need.

Remember that all lenders and investors look for a good business plan, strong financial controls, personal commitment and a well-researched opportunity. Don't be daunted – they need you as much as you need them.

Information needed

Before approaching anyone for finance, you will need to prepare the following information.

☐ Cash flow forecast – showing how much cash will be available in the business and how you will monitor the cash flow.

☐ Balance sheet forecast – showing fixed assets (equipment) and current assets (stock and debtors). This will also indicate how your assets are financed and the expected net worth of the business.

☐ Business plan (see the section below on Writing a Business Plan)

☐ Personal budgets – work out your personal expenditure (mortgage payments, electricity, gas and phone bills). This will show how much money you need to take out of the business.

☐ Forms of identification – any investor will want proof of your identity.

Writing a business plan

Building a business plan will help translate your idea into reality. It may appear very complex at first but in essence it is common sense, based on your objectives, how you can achieve your goals and how to carry all this into an effective plan. It is a roadmap for running your business and should be used as an ongoing tool. You need to build an operational short- medium- and long- term plan and then continually measure your progress against it. As you gather more experience and data, change and improve your plan.

A business plan is not only necessary for raising finance, it has a role to play in everyday business management and at pivotal moments in your business. When you are faced with customer demands, tax deadlines, VAT returns and many other 'business as usual' problems it can seem hard to justify devoting any time at all to drawing up a business plan.

However a business plan makes you analyse the resources you have – finance, people, facilities and premises – to see whether you have enough to reach your end goal. If you don't, not only will you have identified this as a risk, but you can work out how to make up the shortfall. It also makes you research the markets you will compete in both today and tomorrow, helping you to ensure that there is a growing number of customers who will continue to want what you sell. Even if you plan to work alone at first, it's important to cost things and work out how you are going to make any money. Your plan can be used in an application for finance and will help to minimise the risk of failure.

The business plan is normally divided into five major segments: executive summary, business analysis, marketing strategy, management plan and financial projections.

EXECUTIVE SUMMARY

This one-page report highlights the most important points of your business plan with regards to the new business management, services offered, target markets, promotion and financial matters. If finance is sought, the amount should be stated here. The executive summary should appear at the front of your document. It is the introduction and should highlight the attractions of your business.

BUSINESS ANALYSIS

The business analysis explains clearly and concisely the nature of your business and your market. It should detail the form of business, such as sole proprietorship or partnership, the proposed start date, the location, classification and the advisors (normally accountants and lawyers). Give details of the proposed premises, size, location, tenure, costs, next rent review, equipment needed and who your suppliers are likely to be.

MARKET AND INDUSTRY INFORMATION

The market and industry analysis should include information on industry trends, your product, who the target market will be, research data and a brief analysis of the competition. Outline the key characteristics of customers in your target market, such as their age, gender, location and income. Include an outline of your business proposal and the strengths, weaknesses, opportunities and threats (SWOT analysis). Strengths and weaknesses are internal characteristics of your business; opportunities and threats are external.

MANAGEMENT PLAN

The management plan briefly sets out your skills and experience and a record of the people working for you. Detail personnel compensation and benefits, employment policies and procedures.

FINANCIAL PROJECTIONS

This should include profit and cash flow forecasts on a month-by-month basis for the first 12 months. Show how much finance the business might need. Detail how much, when and in what form you need it. State what the finance will be used for. Include an estimate of your personal wealth and survival income.

BUSINESS PLAN TEMPLATES

Many business plans are too long. Keep yours concise, yet comprehensive and well considered. It should be about 12 pages. Include a cover with your document and give it a title and contents page. Make sure it looks professional and is accurate and realistic.

There are many sources available to business people who want information on how to write a detailed plan. Libraries, the internet and most government departments can provide excellent outlines to follow at little or no cost.

Business Link, the Small Business Advice Service (SBAS) and most banks have a business plan template online where all the core elements are clearly set out for you. The sample plan on the SBAS website (www.smallbusinessadvice.org.uk) allows you to fill in the sections and submit the plan to an online advisor for comments. The service will identify an Accredited Business Adviser in your locality who will contact you by email within a day or so and invite you to submit your plan for review.

From the Alliance & Leicester Commercial Bank website (www.alliance-leicestercommercialbank.co.uk), you can download the free Business Planner software. It gives you interactive templates, cash flow forecast, profit and loss forecast, and contains helpful guidance notes right the way through. Alternatively, you may feel better if you consult your own business adviser or accountant.

Top ten tips for writing a business plan
- ☐ Write from your audience's perspective.
- ☐ Include enough detail to ensure the reader has sufficient information to make an informed decision.
- ☐ Research your market thoroughly.
- ☐ Understand the competition.
- ☐ Clearly describe the investment opportunity.
- ☐ Ensure all key areas are covered in the plan.
- ☐ Costs should be documented in full and sales predicted realistically.
- ☐ Include an executive summary.
- ☐ Have it independently reviewed.
- ☐ Detail implementation of the plan.

Approaching business banks

Taking the time to search for the right bank is critical. You should establish a working relationship with a financial institution that provides you with services you need. Look for a bank that markets itself as a lender to small and medium-sized businesses, or for those with a business lending division.

These banking basics should be followed: a limited company must open a business account; sole traders may use their personal current account for business activities. You don't have to choose a business bank account because you are a personal banking customer – they may not offer the best deal for your business. Look for a bank that has a dedicated small business team. The set-up process should be simpler, and dedicated teams will be used to dealing with all types of small businesses and their specific needs. Compare several business banking offerings, and the costs and charges associated with each one. Check the fixed charges the bank may levy on business accounts including transaction fees and overdraft fees. Also see if there is a fee-free period for new customers and what extras the bank offers (for example, credit cards, charge cards, free statements).

When you've done your homework, choose a bank which offers either free banking or zero transaction costs. Ensure the bank offers online business banking so you can check the status of your account day or night. In order to open your account, you will need to provide various documents. Depending on how you are starting up your business, you may also need to provide a business plan.

Government help and support

Research has shown that businesses receiving support and advice are more likely to flourish, gaining competitive advantage and creating high value companies that benefit local communities. Most of this assistance comes from private or third sector providers. However, assistance from the government can help address market failures or equity gaps. Consequently, the government spends £2.5 billion a year in directly supporting businesses to meet the challenges they face, by providing publicly funded grants, subsidies, advice and other support services. Of this, 40% is local funding.

Some companies, particularly time and cash-strapped small and medium-sized businesses, are put off seeking help as a result of confusion over the numerous schemes, multiple providers and a seeming lack of coordination. An annual survey has found that more than 50% of small businesses want government help, but struggle to find their way through the maze of provisions. This means the businesses that will benefit most from support are often those least likely to access it.

Business Link is the single access point for small business advice in England. Businesses are directed to a range of private and public business support options through this central portal. The service is free, impartial and available nationally. Furthermore, you could approach the National Federation of Enterprise Agencies (NFEA), which is a membership body for Local Enterprise Agencies. It forms a network of independent agencies that help small and growing businesses by providing a range of services, such as training, mentoring, provision of loans, incubation and workspace. It operates through the nine UK regions and in turn has nine Regional Development Agencies.

NFEA's Small Business Advice Service (www.smallbusinessadvice.org.uk) provides free and confidential business advice and guidance to anyone planning, starting up or running a small business. A feature of this service is the online Enquiry Service, which can link you directly to one of the 200 or more accredited business advisers. When you submit an enquiry, the service automatically routes it to the most appropriate adviser, based on your postcode. The registration process is simple: just fill in your email address, postcode and an indication of how you found the service. You are then allocated a 4-digit pin number and to log in you simply enter your email address and pin number. The service is totally confidential.

In England, the government has committed itself to the Business Link (www.business link.gov.uk) as a gateway that small businesses can use to access a range of government services.

In Scotland, Scottish Enterprise (www.scottish-enterprise.com) and its local enterprise companies run Business Gateway (www.bgateway.com). They are both funded by the Scottish Executive and involve local councils, local enterprise trusts and other partners. For small businesses in the Highlands and Islands of Scotland, Highlands and Islands Enterprise (www.hie.co.uk) run a similar service. Business Gateway offers assistance in helping small businesses access advice in many areas, including skills development, staff recruitment, sales and marketing, IT and the latest business regulations.

In Wales, the Welsh Assembly Government provides advice and support to businesses through a fully integrated service, Flexible Support for Business (www.business-support-wales.gov.uk). It provides fast, simple and straightforward access to information, dedicated relationship managers, funding and specialist support.

In Northern Ireland, services for small businesses are provided by Invest NI (www.investni.com) and local enterprise agencies located in each of the council areas.

GRANTS

Grants are not that easy to come by and you will need very specific plans for the business you are seeking to fund. It is extremely rare for a grant to finance 100% of the costs of any project. Grants typically cover 15% to 50% of the total finance required. There are many different grant schemes in existence. Identify the grants your business could be eligible for and talk to the administrators of any grant schemes that seem to fit your situation.

You must have a clear plan and it is likely that you will need to show how the project ties in with the strategic direction of your business as outlined in your business plan. It is probably worth paying for professional help to apply for any grants worth £50,000 or more. Experts can help you to model your venture so that it is more likely to meet the qualifying criteria for the grant. Some accountants and consultants are recognised grant experts.

A grant application can be lengthy and can take months to process, so make sure you plan well in advance. Also note that certain types of expenditure are not eligible for grants, such as working capital, interest charges, road-going vehicles, rent costs and hired assets bought through an operating lease.

You should also contact your local Business Link or other business support organisations. Basic information is usually free. Most have access to the European Information Centre and to Grantfinder, a database which will identify appropriate European, national and government grant schemes. There is a grant search facility at Business Gateway in Scotland (www.btgateway.com) and Business Eye (www.businesseye.org.uk) in Wales can offer help and advice.

Business Link's Grants and Support Directory is an online database that you can use to search for potential sources of help either at the start-up phase of your business or to help with further business development. It is an extensive database that includes information on grant and support schemes from central and local government as well as through private organisations.

The website www.j4bgrants.co.uk gives comprehensive government grant information for the UK and Ireland and other sources of funding for your business. It has more than 4,500 financial programmes researched with daily updates. Simply register for free and start searching.

Says Amanda Hartley of Amanda's Blue Orchid Florist in Hull:

> *Money was my biggest issue. I opened my shop when I was 19 and was turned away by most financial organisations. Youth Enterprise in Hull helped me with lots of advice and gave me £500. It wasn't much but clearly they thought that giving me a grant would help me – they had faith in me.*

Setting up an accounting system

There are numerous accounting software programs and most will perform basic bookkeeping functions, such as tracking expenditures, taxes collected, receivables, and invoice generation. You should talk to other shop owners about accounting software to determine which program will best suit your needs. A computerised system can automate routine tasks. Some software companies have a trial version available and many dealers have demonstration programs at their store. Choose software that can handle sales, invoicing and receipts; purchases and payments; banking and cash management; VAT, tax and accounts; stock control and payroll.

Well-known packages include the following.

- ☐ Microsoft Money Business and Personal – performs all day-to-day accounting functions, as well as generating up-to-date tax positions and quarterly reports. Costs about £50, including VAT (www.microsoft.com/money).

- ☐ Mind Your Own Business (MYOB) – offers software designed for small businesses. First Accounts is a package for start-ups and the self-employed, while MYOB Accounting is more fully featured. Costs from £199, excluding VAT (www.myob.co.uk).

- ☐ QuickBooks – offers all day-to-day functions, along with customisable invoicing and supplier tracking, and an electronic invoicing and payment facility. Costs from £50, including VAT (www.quickbooks.co.uk).

- ☐ Sage Software – offers a variety of accounting software solutions for many kinds of business. Five core packages can be augmented with additional modules to suit the individual firm's needs. Costs from £109, including VAT (www.sage.com).

☐ Simply Books – designed as an easy-to-use package specifically for very small businesses and sole traders. It offers all the standard bookkeeping facilities, as well as VAT processing and analysis. Costs from £100, including VAT (www.simplybooks.net).

Once your systems are in place, you need to monitor your performance. You should use the information you have gathered to compare your actual figures against your projections. They will hardly ever match exactly, but if there is a significant difference, you will need to find the reason and decide what to do about it.

Real world budgeting

No one knows what the future holds but budgeting in your business can help you to anticipate problems, improve your ability to control your retail business and reduce the level of uncertainty. Your budgets should be realistic, but without previous figures as a guide it is a bit of a stab into thin air.

When you prepare your budget, you need to include the fixed costs of running your shop (rent, rates, insurance, utility charges, wages, interest charges and advertising) which do not vary each month or depend on the level of your sales. With these fixed costs you can calculate what volume of sales you need to break even, as follows:

$$£ \text{ breakeven} = \frac{£ \text{ fixed costs} \times 100}{\% \text{ gross margin}}$$

So, if your gross margin is 25%, sales must be four times as large as fixed costs to break even. Then include variable costs (materials, distribution, equipment), which will vary with sales. Semi-variable costs contain both fixed and variable elements.

ASSESSING SALES

Now you need to estimate your sales forecasts, based on what you expect your future sales to be, keeping in mind the calculation above. Variations in sales will be reflected on how you price and market your product, changes in the retail sector, changes in your business, the launch of new products and what your competitors are doing. Assess what you could do to accumulate more sales. This could possibly mean contacting potential customers, advertising, promotions directed at existing customers, and seasonal patterns in your business and the retail sector. Prepare a 12-month forecast and update it on a monthly basis linking it to your cash budget (cash flow forecast) using actual figures from the previous month.

These expenditure and sales forecasts are used to prepare your budgets. The cash flow forecast uses the expenditure and sales budgets to forecast the money going into and out of your bank account each month. Prepare profit and loss and balance sheet budgets. The profit and loss budget shows your projected profits for the 12-month period. The balance sheet budget shows your projected balance sheet at the end of this period.

Once analysed, your budgets give you the chance to deal with potential problems before they happen and to identify business peaks and troughs. Your cash budget projects your future cash position month by month. Profit and loss budgets let you analyse projected margins and other important ratios. Your projected balance sheet allows you to analyse stock turnover and other significant figures. Preparing forecasts for the relevant information means you can budget for and analyse any of your main performance indicators.

It is easier to analyse the potential effects of changes to your budget assumptions if you use forecasting software. It will indicate the effects on your cash flow, profits and balance sheet. Compare your actual income with your sales budget every month and analyse the reasons for any shortfalls in turnover or if the turnover is higher than budgeted. Compare the timing of income with your projections. Analysing these differences will help you to improve your ability to set future budgets and allow you to take appropriate action.

You can carry out basic budgeting procedures, but if you do not have a financial disposition you should get help preparing balance and profit and loss sheets. Most banks supply software free or charge but if you intend to buy a forecasting package, Sage's Winforecast is quite user-friendly. Alternatively, you can get training from your local Business Link or relevant software manufacturer.

Women in business

A new £25-million equity fund for women-led businesses has been launched. The Aspire Investment Fund, reportedly the first of its kind in the UK, will offer women who own businesses or who have entrepreneurial ideas the chance to secure financial support. Women have been massively under-represented in UK enterprise. They account for 50% of the adult population and working population and yet only 15% of business owners are women. However, in terms of percentage growth women outperformed in comparison to the national average and overtook men. Female-only start-ups increased by 9% to more than 90,000 in 2008 compared to 83,000 in 2007.

4
DETERMINING THE COSTS

Once you have created your business plan, you can determine the costs involved in starting your new business. Determine your obvious and hidden costs so that you know how much it will cost to begin. Calculate the costs over a period of six months because it often takes that long to make a profit after paying these costs.

The obvious outlays are the cost of any building you will need, whether you lease, rent or buy, and utilities such as water, gas and electricity. Take into account the cost of any merchandise or products that you will need before you can open shop. Add in the cost of any vehicle you might need (repayments, insurance, road tax), public liability insurance and your own national insurance contributions.

Then there are other variable costs to factor in, such as telephone, accountancy fees, stationery, postage, bank charges, advertising and marketing material. Factor in your optional costs, such as redecoration and refitting, repairs and renewals, signage, staff wages and your own drawings/wages.

 On average, wages account for a business's biggest expense, representing nearly 29% of outgoings. This is followed by investment in stock and materials at 17.5%, tax at 16%, with fuel costs accounting for 10%.

Insurance matters

For the majority of small businesses, public liability insurance is the most important type of cover. It protects a business by covering the cost of a claim if an accident happens with a member of the public, resulting in injury or damage to them or their property. Claims for public liability can run into tens of thousands of pounds. If your business employs staff, even on a part-time or temporary basis, you must by law have employers' liability insurance. You are legally obliged to have a minimum of £5 million cover. If an employee is injured or becomes ill in the course of their work, and it can be proven to be the fault of your business, you could face a claim for compensation. An employers' liability policy will ensure that your business is protected from this cost.

According to a recent report by the Federation of Small Businesses (FSB), almost six out of ten small businesses fall victim to crime each year, with those in the north of England and in urban areas most likely to be targeted. You should, therefore, insure your stock and cash left on the premises with a specific insurance to protect it from theft, damage or destruction. You may also wish to include business interruption insurance under your policy. This cover compensates your business for lost income when it is forced to suspend work due to an event that is stated in your policy. It could be for a burglary, a fire on your premises, or even due to police temporarily closing your business for a crime investigation.

SELECTING THE RIGHT POLICY FOR YOUR BUSINESS

There seems to be a lot of choice when it comes to cover, but most insurers will include all of them under one policy. This not only makes it easier when the time comes to renew, but it can also cut down the cost of your insurance. When you come to make the decision about what insurance to take out, it is worthwhile paying a visit to a comparison website, for example www.SimplyBusiness.co.uk. These sites allow businesses of any size to easily compare prices from a variety of insurers, and check actual policy working to ensure the correct cover has been chosen.

Once you have selected your insurance company, answer all the questions in full and disclose any relevant factors concerning your business when completing the proposal form. Failure to do so may entitle the insurer to treat the policy as invalid. Your insurer will help you work out what level of cover you need. You can either pay a lump sum or you can spread the costs by paying a smaller amount each month. Be sure to check the interest rate charged. You may also be able to save money by buying cover that lasts for more than a year.

You can check if the organisation or person you deal with is authorised by looking at the Financial Services Authority's site at www.fsa.gov.uk. More information is also available from the British Insurance Brokers' Association (www.biba.org.uk), Financial Ombudsman Service (FOS, www.financial-ombudsman.org.uk) and the Institute of Insurance Brokers (IIB, www.iib-uk.com).

Finding suitable premises

Location can play a decisive role in determining the success or failure of your shop. The goal is to get the best location for the money you have available. The decision on where to locate should be based on the quality of services in that area, easy access, and nearby businesses that could help to draw potential customers to your shop. However, firstly determine how much retail space, storage area and/or size of office you will need.

Next, examine the kind of products you intend to sell: will your shop be considered a speciality shop, a convenience store or a designer outlet? Specialty goods are more distinctive than most products and customers generally won't mind travelling out of the way to purchase your wares. It may also do well near other specialty stores.

Convenience goods require easy access, allowing the customer to make a purchase quickly. Therefore, a shopping centre would not be a good location for convenience goods. This product type is bought by a wide range of customers and is lower priced.

A designer outlet usually sells higher-priced items that are bought infrequently by the customer. Because the prices of theses items are higher, this type of customer will want to compare prices before making a purchase. Therefore, retailers will do well to locate their shop near similar businesses.

Says Anian Schmitt of Only Roses in London:

> *Your location should be evaluated very carefully. For us, a rose shop on the high street is not the best place to be. We therefore chose the heart of a residential area, on a highly frequented road, where it is more convenient to stop and buy flowers.*

If you are choosing a city or rural area to locate your retail shop, research the area thoroughly before making a final decision. Read local papers and speak to other small businesses in the area. Obtain location demographics from the local library, Regional Development Agency, local council, or Chamber of Commerce. You know who your customers are, so make sure you find a location where your customers live, work and shop.

You will want to be located where there are many shoppers, but only if such shoppers meet the definition of your target market. Small retail shops often benefit from the traffic of nearby larger stores. You'll need to study how many people walk or drive past the location, whether there is public transport to the area, whether customers and delivery vehicles get in and out of the parking area easily, and whether there is adequate parking.

Also consider the visibility of your shop from a shopper's point of view. Your shop should be easily seen from the main flow of traffic and your signage clearly visible. It is possible that better visibility can mean you'll need to budget less cash for advertising. Don't feel rushed into making a decision on where to site your business. Take your time, research the area and have patience.

These are important questions to ask yourself about your desired location:
- ☐ Which is your target area?
- ☐ How expensive is the area?
- ☐ Prime town centre location or out-of-town business park?
- ☐ Where are your potential customers?
- ☐ Where is there least competition, or should you be near to similar businesses?
- ☐ Should you be close to specialist suppliers?
- ☐ Must you be near transport links (motorway, railway station or bus stop)?
- ☐ Can your customers and employees reach the premises easily?
- ☐ Will you be able to get supplies and make deliveries easily?
- ☐ What local facilities do you need? For instance, do you need to be near a bank, post office or local parking?
- ☐ How important is the image you project?
- ☐ What impression will visitors form?

Personal contacts may know of suitable premises or suggest other people to consult. Premises are also advertised online, in local newspapers and property magazines. *Daltons Weekly* (www.daltons.co.uk) covers property across the UK. Business Link, commercial property agents or your local council will also be able to advise you.

Says Amanda Hartley of Amanda's Blue Orchid Florist in Hull:

> ❛ *Finding the right premises was a nightmare! I really struggled to find something that was realistic in size as well as rental – it's hard when you see an empty shop to imagine it containing all the products you envisage. I'm lucky that my shop is on a busy street and has its own frontage, which is very important for selling plants. Parking is a very big draw to any shop, as well as bus stops (there's one right outside my shop) and a bike rack. The pitfalls are contracts – you have to go through them with a very fine toothcomb and solicitors cost a fortune too. I had problems with agencies – they didn't get the forms to me in time, which meant I missed out on my dream location. Honestly, though, if I had opened there I wouldn't have lasted – everything happens for a reason.* ❜

If you use a commercial property agency, give them a detailed spec. Decide on the size you will need, any special needs, your maximum price including VAT, and any annual charges. Property size is usually calculated on a square footage rate, so work out how much space you will need and base your search on that.

Once you have found the right place, you may need to carry out a survey of the structural state of the building. The Royal Institute of Chartered Surveyors will advise you on surveyors in your area. When renting, you will normally be expected to pay your landlord's, solicitor's and surveyor's fees.

Also check the property grading and see if you will be able to do renovations, if there is any history of subsidence or damp, and whether there has been any flooding in the area. Ask your solicitor to request a flood report from an environmental company, which provides information about flood areas, such as Groundsure, Landmark and Homecheck. Make sure you are on the right side of complicated regulations, such as environment health rules. Bear in mind that your premises should be accessible to customers who are disabled. The building will have to meet disability discrimination laws and health and safety regulations.

Regional facts and figures

There are nine Regional Development Agencies (RDAs) in England. Here are some of their insights into why you should locate your business in their region.

NORTHWEST REGIONAL DEVELOPMENT AGENCY (NWDA)

Over the last two years, 4,282 businesses started up in the North West. 17% are classified as retail. This region has a large population and key urban centres which are able to support a diverse retail trade. Many towns attract high levels of spending from outside catchment areas. Chester, Carlisle and Southport are typical examples. Many parts of the region also have wealthy residents with significant purchasing power, including Cheshire, some suburbs in Manchester, Formby, Southport, parts of the Fylde Coast, such as Lytham St Annes, the Ribble Valley and West Wirral. Business support in the North West is offered through the Intensive Start-up Service, Start-up Service, and High Growth Support programmes. Contact the NWDA (www.nwda.co.uk) for more information.

ONE NORTHEAST

The retail and wholesale sector is important to the North East, making up about 23% of the business base. About 1,000 businesses register in this sector each year (based on most recent VAT registrations). For more precise information contact One NorthEast (www.onenortheast.co.uk).

EAST MIDLANDS DEVELOPMENT AGENCY

At the start of 2008 there were 29,700 VAT registered businesses in the wholesale, retail and repairs sector of the East Midlands, accounting for 21% of all VAT registered businesses in the region. The retail sector has experienced a slight decline in recent years, falling from 24% in 2000 to its current level.

The highest rentals for retail space are charged in Nottingham, although there has been a slight reduction in the rentals charged for prime location premises between 2004 and 2008. Leicester has experienced the largest growth in rentals for prime location premises over the same time period. This reflects the completion of a substantial development of retail space in the area, increasing the attractiveness of the area's shopping experience.

Mansfield has the lowest rental values for the three types of retail premises. This is a result of its lower resident population relative to other urban centres and lack of sizeable retail locations.

Businesses in the East Midlands, along with the rest of the UK, have obviously been affected by the current recession. Consumer expenditure in the region remains relatively flat, continuing to impact on retailers and other sectors such as hotels and restaurants. However, although the East Midlands' economy is still contracting, following a sharp downturn at the end of 2008, there are signs that expectations are beginning to improve, with some evidence suggesting that businesses in the region have a more positive outlook. More information is available from the East Midlands Development Agency (www.emda.org.uk).

Retail businesses, as with all businesses in the East Midlands, can access a complete range of support from Business Link to help them develop and grow through the Business Link service. Business Link provides help for those entrepreneurs who are looking to start up new ventures, as well as for those who are already running a business.

SOUTH WEST OF ENGLAND REGIONAL DEVELOPMENT AGENCY

The South West generates 9% of the total output in England and its gross domestic product (GDP) outstrips the national average. The region has Britain's highest business survival rates. It has a population of five million people, equivalent to 8.6% of Britain's population. Cities are modern, vibrant and thriving and include Bath, Bournemouth, Poole, Exeter, Gloucester, Swindon and Bristol – the UK's most affluent and economically successful city after London.

The South West of England Regional Development Agency provides a number of bespoke information fact sheets that outline key steps involved in setting up a retail business in the region. It also runs a series of start-up workshops, covering three themed areas of planning and finance, sales and marketing, and finance and accounts. More information is available from the South West RDA (www.southwestrda.org.uk).

EAST OF ENGLAND DEVELOPMENT AGENCY

The East of England's rate of business registration is almost on a par with the national average, but significant disparities in performance exist within the region. In 2008 there were 259,050 enterprises in the region that were registered for VAT and/or PAYE (National Insurance). Historically, enterprise survival rates in the East of England have been high. Women's rate of entrepreneurship in the region is level with the UK average. However, women are more likely to let barriers hinder their enterprise success and enterprise survival. Areas in the region that are considered deprived across a range of measures also have lower rates of enterprise formation than average.

The East of England Development Agency (EEDA) does not see the retail sector as a key sector to drive economic growth, but is aware of the needs of shopkeepers to the extent that all small and medium-sized businesses require a good balance of vibrant economy and appropriate place and infrastructure to flourish.

The three Support for Business programmes (Intensive Start-up Service, Start-up Service and High Growth Support) can also be accessed through the regional Business Link. EEDA also funds some specific programmes aimed at correcting market failures specific to the region, or that are not funded out of national schemes. More information on the region is available from EEDA (www.eeda.org.uk).

LONDON DEVELOPMENT AGENCY

Greater London is the smallest of the nine English regions but with a population of 7.2 million it is the largest city in Europe. London tends to have annual net inflows of people from outside the UK, with almost 30% of London's population from a minority ethnic group. London has more than 40,000 shops and some 80 individual markets, including Walthamstow Market, Europe's longest daily street market. The West End has the largest retail area in the UK. Oxford Street alone has more than 300 shops.

Business Link in London (BLiL) is the primary gateway through which businesses can be connected to the services that meet their needs. A summary of business support products offered by the LDA include:

- ☐ Business Link in London (BliL, www.businesslink.gov.uk/london);
- ☐ Business London (www.lda.gov.uk);
- ☐ British Library Business & IP Centre (www.bl.uk/bipc/index);
- ☐ Gateway to Investment (g2i, www.g2i.org);
- ☐ Community Development Finance Institutions (CDFIs, www.lda.gov.uk).

OTHER REGIONS

Information on the three remaining regions is available from:

- ☐ South East England Development Agency (www.seeda.co.uk);
- ☐ Yorkshire Forward (www.yorkshire-forward.com);
- ☐ Advantage West Midlands (www.advantagewm.co.uk).

Signing a lease

Before signing a lease, be sure you understand all the rules, policies and procedures related to your retail shop location. Contact your local authority for information on regulations regarding signage. Ask about any restrictions that may affect your retail operation and any future planning that could change traffic, such as road closures. Check any hidden costs, such as security, rates and service charges, insurance premiums, and your local council's business rates. Lawyers for Business (www.lawsociety.org.uk/choosingandusing/helpyourbusiness/foryourbusiness.law) provide 30 minutes of free legal advice on premises and leases.

Says Anian Schmitt of Only Roses in London:

> *The only pitfall we found with our lease agreement was that it took ages (three months) to finalise and was very expensive in terms of legal costs.*

The advantages of leasing may only become apparent as your business becomes more established. For small start-up businesses, the pros and cons are usually finely balanced. However, with leasing you have a wider choice as most business property is leased. In addition, you will have a certain sense of security, with the right to stay there for the length of the lease (usually 3 to 25 years). Short (five year) leases are the current trend. Usually, you can improve the property (subject to obtaining written consent from the landlord) and landlords may offer incentives to take up a lease, possibly a rent-free period.

There are disadvantages though. Bad landlords or odd clauses in the lease can cause grievances. You may need to move on as your business changes. In this case, most leases can be passed on to a new tenant, but you may still be liable for rent and costs (including the legal costs for both sides) if the new tenant fails to pay up. In some cases, you may also be responsible for all repairs. Most leases allow the rent to be increased periodically (every three or five years), in line with market rents.

CODE FOR LEASING BUSINESS PREMISES

A new Commercial Lease Code was launched in March 2007 and aims to redress the balance of power between landlord and tenant. This code of practice helps to make leasing shops and offices more user-friendly for small businesses. The code is in three parts: the Landlord Code, the Occupier Guide, and Model Heads of Terms. However, it is the Landlord Code section which will have the most impact on you – it provides guidance in ten basic areas including lease negotiations, rent deposits, break clauses, rent review, alterations, disposals and service charges.

With regard to lease negotiations, landlords are recommended by the code to make offers in writing which clearly state the main terms of the lease, including the rent, the length of the term and any break rights, whether or not tenants will have security of tenure, the rent review arrangements, rights to dispose of the property and repairing obligations. Moreover, landlords must promote flexibility, stating whether alternative lease terms are available, and must propose rents for different lease terms if requested by prospective tenants.

SERVICE CHARGES

With regard to service charges, landlords must, during negotiations, provide best estimates of service charges, insurance payments and any other outgoings that tenants will incur under their leases. They are recommended to disclose known events that would impact on the amount of future service charges.

A right to break a lease early is important to tenants as it gives them flexibility. Historically, landlords have insisted on break clauses hedged around with onerous conditions which often made it difficult to exercise the break effectively. The pre-conditions recommended by the code, however, are limited, and thankfully are usually easy to satisfy.

The code can be a useful tool for tenants negotiating new leases. Compliance with the code is currently voluntary but, even if the draft lease produced by the landlord's lawyers is not expressed to be code-compliant, a well-prepared tenant's lawyer can often invoke the code provisions as evidence of good practice in a particular area. This can be enough to persuade landlords to change their minds and relax their terms. Indeed landlords who show willingness to enter into the spirit of the code at the outset may well find it easier to encourage tenants to sign up leases in their buildings in the first place.

 Alarm Bell

Beware of leases that cannot be transferred or sold.

The tenant/landlord relationship can be fraught with dangers. One of the greatest is dilapidations: the obligation you have to keep the landlord's property in a good state of repair. If you sign a lease without checking the dilapidations terms you could be in for big –

and expensive – problems. The extent to which you can be obliged to repair the building you occupy can vary significantly from lease to lease. However, whether you take on a full repairing covenant or negotiate a lesser obligation with the landlord, it is likely that you will face a dilapidations claim at some point.

When negotiating the terms of a lease, landlords are keen to obtain a 'clear' lease under which the tenant bears the cost of all repairs so that any rent charged is essentially pure profit. However, you will want to limit your repairing liabilities, especially if taking a short-term lease.

REPAIRS TO YOUR PREMISES

Leases of entire buildings often contain full-repair covenants, which mean that the tenant is responsible for carrying out and paying for all internal, external, structural and non-structural repairs. Leases of part of a building normally contain an 'internal' repairing covenant under which the landlord has to repair the external areas, common and structural parts (normally recovering the cost via service charges), while the tenant is responsible for the internal part of their premises.

If you have taken a lease of part of a building, you must be careful to ensure that the internal repairing covenant and the definitions in the lease are accurate and that the lease makes it clear who is responsible for repairing each part of the building. The precise meaning of the word 'repair' has caused many a dispute. The best way to avoid unexpected dilapidations is for you to understand the nature of the repairing obligation you are accepting at the outset. This means arranging a building survey and fully understanding what the lease requires.

A consortium of business, property, finance and legal organisations created the guide, *The Code of Leasing Business Premises in England and Wales*, to avoid the pitfalls of lease agreements, ensuring landlords operate to a pan-industry agreed standard. For full details, see www.leasingbusinesspremises.co.uk

Buying a property

Few small businesses choose to purchase premises because it ties up cash, which is generally needed as working capital. You usually need cash for 30% of the property's price and a commercial mortgage for the other 70%. The advantages include owning the freehold until you choose to sell the property. There should be no large increases in your monthly outgoings (whereas rents can increase significantly). You can alter and improve the premises as much as you like. It is a good long-term investment.

The disadvantages come really from the major financial commitment you have to make. Maybe you would be better off keeping the money for running the business. Unless you have extra cash, and will not need the money in future years, buying a property may not be the right decision. Your property may be costly to maintain and values go up and down all the time.

Rents, rates and utilities

Rent is usually one of your biggest costs. For the past couple of years, landlords have had the upper hand as commercial rents have risen ever higher but balance of power is shifting and you may be able to negotiate a better deal. Your negotiating strength will depend on the demand for property in certain areas.

Rents are usually paid in advance on the four quarter days in the year which are traditionally 25 March, 24 June, 29 September and 25 December. You may able to persuade your landlord to agree to a variation to the rent payment dates and switch to monthly rather than quarterly.

RATES

Business rates are often the third largest expenditure item after wages and rent for small businesses. They are set by your local authority and are payable annually, although most authorities will allow payment in ten monthly instalments. Business rates increase annually in April and are calculated on the Retail Price Index (RPI) of the preceding September. In England, the standard multiplier for 2009/10 is 48.5 (different multipliers are used for Wales, Scotland and Northern Ireland). So, if your property has a rateable value of £10,000 it is charged at £4,850. The rateable value is based on the likely annual open market rent for the premises at a set date.

In England and Wales, small businesses are entitled to small business rate relief if the rateable value of the premises is less than £15,000 (£21,500 in London). In Northern Ireland, there is a hardship relief scheme for small businesses that came into operation on 31 December 2005. Certain businesses in the countryside can also qualify, such as those in small villages with a population under 3,000. You can qualify for a 50% reduction in the rates bill if you are the only village general store. Business ratepayers who are eligible have to apply for the relief each year. You have to send in your application for the relief to your local authority within six months of the end of the financial year to which the relief applies.

Details of the rateable value of your premises and how it has been calculated can be viewed at the Valuation Office Agency (VOA) www.voa.gov.uk and the Scottish Assessors Association (SAA) www.saa.gov.uk.

UTILITIES

When deciding on your utility providers, make sure you understand their full tariff policies. All the utility companies have become much more competitive, so it might be worth shopping around to see which would be the cheapest. You will be billed every quarter.

Telephone

According to recent studies, more than 60% of small firms in the UK spend in excess of £300 a month on fixed line calls and £400 a month on mobile phone calls. Most businesses that move away from BT do so on the basis of improved rates from a competitor. Be aware of things like call set-up fees, minimum call charges, headline rates and rounding up calls.

You can also save money on the line itself. Most suppliers now offer a 5–15% discount on line rental versus the BT standard rate. Bear in mind that the lines are exactly the same as with BT Retail, it is just that they are supplied by BT Wholesale. Most decent-sized alternative suppliers will be a BT Wholesale partner and in a position to manage your lines just as well as BT themselves.

Look out for a supplier who is a member of the Federation of Communication Service Providers (FCS), the industry body that ensures members adhere to strict sales and marketing and customer service codes, as well as adhering to Ofcom (the telecoms regulator) regulations.

Voice Over IP (VoIP)

Research also shows that small and medium-sized enterprises (SMEs) that switched over to VoIP experienced, on average, a 23% reduction in overheads and a 13% fall in IT expenses. VoIP is Voice Over IP – encoding your telephone conversation and sending it over the internet instead of tying up a phone line for one conversation.

The most common example of VoIP is Skype but a problem with Skype is that it is tied to your computer. Other VoIP business options are designed to work on computers, sit-on-your-desk phone sets, and with PBX systems from one-line-two-extensions to multi-line hundreds of extensions. By routing calls via the internet you save money on each call, while a call to another VoIP user is free. However, if you make heavy use of VoIP you may need to increase your broadband speed or even add a second broadband line for voice calls because calls use up internet bandwidth. If you only make a few calls, you should have enough spare bandwidth from a sensibly sized connection for one or two calls at least.

Popular UK providers that can meet the internet telephony needs of a small business include Skype, Call Union, PlusTalk, Vonage and Tesco. The greatest benefit of using these packages is that, where two locations are equipped with the same service, the calls are free.

Initial charges vary according to the provider but Vonage charges £7.99 monthly rental with a £9.99 set-up fee and £8.99 for equipment delivery. Calls are free to all landlines in the UK and Ireland. With Skype you pay £2.24 monthly subscription and calls to landlines in the UK and Ireland are charged at about 1p per minute. You can buy a USB cordless phone for less than £15 and also have incoming Skype calls forwarded to your mobile phone.

By comparison, a standard BT landline, not a VoIP service, costs £10.50 a month plus £124.99 for installation of the phone line. Call charges vary depending on your payment plan. You are billed every quarter for the calls you have made, plus an amount for the line rental for the next quarter.

Broadband

Having an internet presence is essential to carry out your daily business tasks and transactions and your broadband is the key to that. A reliable business broadband service is invaluable when running your business. It offers faster download speeds and support. However, an unreliable connection can cost valuable time and money. Ensure your monthly download limits are suitable for your business needs. You should also check out the security features that come with your broadband package, such as virus protection.

Most business broadband providers offer a free domain name and a static Internet Protocol (IP) address. A domain name allows you to create your own name, which helps you build both credibility and market awareness. A static IP address allows you to access your PC from anywhere in the country and to run your own email server, web server and private network.

A typical package, such as UK Online's Business Broadband Package (www.ukonline.net) costs from £19.99 a month (plus VAT) and comes with a free connection for a limited period. It has a 8Mb connection; unlimited service; a UK-based 24/7 freephone for technical support; up to 20 email addresses with domain name, webmail and spam filter; and free McAfee Security for 12 months.

Other general expenses

Every month you can expect to spend money on a variety of things for your business, for example:

☐ business stationery – letterheads, business cards, invoices and other miscellaneous stationery items are important for the image and efficiency of your shop. Your local printer will be able to give you an estimate on how much each will cost;

☐ postage – you are likely to spend a certain amount on a regular basis, but every now and then you might decide to do a mail shot advertising your business;

☐ window cleaner – you may wish to have your windows cleaned daily, or maybe just once or twice a week;

☐ repairs and maintenance – you will have to have regular maintenance to maintain high standards for health and safety. Make sure you have a reliable maintenance person as leaks occur, heating breaks down, tiles crack and hinges come off doors. Alternatively, take out a contract with a plumber, electrician and heating engineer. It could save you money in the long run. Furthermore, for advice on structure and repairs use a qualified surveyor who is a member of the Royal Institution of Chartered Surveyors (www.rics.org);

☐ membership to trade association – joining one of the professional bodies will cost you an annual membership fee. These range in price, but most will include a copy of their trade magazine;

☐ subscription to a trade journal – for trade publications, see Further Reading at the end of this book.

Buying stock

Considerable thought needs to go into the type of products you are going to stock. Once you have decided on your product base, pick out suppliers you believe can offer the quality of product and service you need. To work out initial costs, ask your selected suppliers to send you product details, price lists and other relevant information. Many vendors and suppliers will send catalogues only with dealer price lists to established businesses. A few may share this information if you explain to them you are planning a new business. Don't be afraid to shop around for the best deals.

Reliability, quality, service and value for money should all be taken into consideration when choosing suppliers. Get quotes, including details such as discounts and payment terms. Ask how often prices will rise, what influences will cause them to rise, and how you will be notified. Specify what you want and agree details, proposing your own terms. But don't squeeze a supplier if you plan to buy regularly from that source.

BUILDING GOOD RELATIONSHIPS

By building a good relationship with your suppliers, you will save money and time in the long run. It may even improve the quality of goods you receive. Understand how your suppliers work and discuss with them whether a contract or service level agreement (SLA) is necessary. A guide to purchasing strategies, including improving supplier quality and reliability, removing risk and saving yourself time and money is available from the Buying Support Agency, www.buyingsupport.co.uk

Agree payment terms so there are no future disputes. Payments in advance should generally be avoided, especially if you are unsure about the supplier's credit-worthiness. For convenience, it is best to set up accounts with your main suppliers. Ask for a discount for early settlement, retrospective rebates or volume discounts. Remember that holding stock ties up money, so aim to minimise your stock levels and make delivery of supplies the supplier's responsibility. The Law Society (www.lawsociety.org.uk) has useful information on contracts with suppliers on their website.

Make delivery terms clear when you place your contract. Always check what has actually been delivered before you sign the delivery note. For small shops, a weekly stock check and ordering routine should be sufficient. Devise your own system but keep accurate records of all purchases. Suppliers are easy enough to find but spend time on research. You can then ask around, check with the trade associations, look at trade journals, enquire at your local Chamber of Commerce and Business Link, visit exhibitions and trade fairs and browse through directories, such as www.yell.com, www.thelocalweb.net or www.scoot.co.uk

Choosing your fittings

When deciding what fittings and displays to purchase, find a wholesaler that has a full range of shopfittings, good service, a price guarantee, cost effective delivery, accepts major credit cards, a quotation service, a contact line and an online catalogue.

The following list provides you with an idea of what may be needed across retail categories (prices are a guide only).

- A boards, from £65.
- Acrylic displays (for jewellery, china, giftware, hats, scarves), from £1.50.
- Bodyforms and mannequins, from £115.
- Card and giftwrap displays, from £130.
- Cash registers, from £87.
- Clothes displays and rails, from £20.
- Coat hangers (metal, plastic, wood, bridal, lingerie, trouser), from 58p.
- Counters, from £178.
- Display stands, pedestals (rotating, tiered, wooden), from £30.
- Gridwall panels, from £22.
- In-store security – security mirrors, from £52; changing room discs, from 58p; garment locks, from £6; counterfeit note detectors, from £21; decoy cameras, from £15.
- Packaging – bubble wrap, from £6; budget paper bags, from £3.50; garment bags, from £3.50; gift boxes, from £12; plastic/paper carrier bags, from £9; tissue paper, from £6.50.
- Pricing and tagging guns, from £3.
- Rails, from £23.
- Shelving and gondolas, from £130.
- Shopping baskets (plastic, wicker and wire), from £5.
- Wire card and leaflet displays, from £67.

When buying or leasing equipment, think through the following.

- Technical specifications.
- Compatibility with other equipment.
- Power supply.
- Guarantees.
- Technical support.
- Options for expansion and upgrading.
- Purchase price.
- Delivery and installation costs.
- Maintenance costs.
- Running costs.

Be careful with long maintenance contracts. Read the small print carefully and ask your supplier to explain your present and future commitments.

You may decide to lease some items and one advantage of a leasing agreement is that the cost can be spread over a period, which will help your cash flow. Generally, the payments are fixed at the beginning of the lease period and paid monthly. Ownership of the equipment remains with the leasing company, although you will more than likely be responsible for maintenance. Your equipment supplier may offer leasing facilities but, if not, contact the Finance and Leasing Association (www.fla.org.uk) who will give you a list of those that do.

OFFICE SUPPLIES

In addition, you will need such office supplies as documentation books, markers and pens, notebooks, pins and clips, staplers, till rolls and other sundries. You will also need point of sale materials, including:

- adhesive tickets, from £4;
- clearance tickets, from £1.65;
- dayglo cards, from £1.30;
- pricing cards, from 75p;
- sale posters, from 65p;
- sale tickets, from £1.90;
- string tickets, from £8;
- tagging, from 23p.

You will also need to purchase an electronic cash till, for recording and storing payments, a chip and PIN machine, and a computer. You could try the following suppliers:

- Crown Display, Kestrel Court Business Park, Harbour Road, Portishead, North Somerset BS20 7AN, tel: 0800-587 5880, email: sales@crowndisplay.co.uk, www.crowndisplay.co.uk

- EquipAShop, 16 Prince Regent Road, Belfast BT5 6QR, tel: 028-9079 9990, email: Sales@EquipAShop.com, www.equipashop.com (online catalogue and pricing available)

- Retail Equipment Sales and Services Ltd, Unit 12 Westgate, Everite Road, Widnes, Cheshire WA8 8RA, tel: 0151-420 2147, email: sales@retaileqquipment.co.uk, www.retailequipment.co.uk

- Total Shop Solutions, 19 Cunliffe Drive, Kettering NN16 8LD, tel: 01536-5227000, www.totalshopsolutions.co.uk

Contactless payment systems have been launched in London and are set to roll out all over the UK by 2012. These payment systems allow customers to wave their credit or debit card in front of the scanner and immediate payment of up to £10 is made. Speed at the till is reduced dramatically, and for this reason the technology has already been embraced by high-traffic sectors such as coffee shops and fast food outlets.

Employing and training staff

Employees are one of the biggest assets in any business. Finding the right person quickly and at the right price is not always as easy as it seems. Traditional methods of advertising can be expensive and ineffective for small businesses whereas advertising a vacancy on a recruitment website may be a more cost-effective solution to your recruitment needs.

Before you begin the hiring process, take a moment to make sure you really need the help. Remember that you can reduce your workload by outsourcing some parts of your business that would be better served by a professional. Bookkeeping, marketing and information technology are areas that could be outsourced.

In addition, hiring staff can be expensive. Keep in mind that you will need to pay at least the minimum hourly wage and you will also have taxes and workers' compensation to pay. However, an extra employee may generate enough new sales to more than compensate for their salary. The additional help could give you a chance to produce more products or serve more customers efficiently. If the added business does not outweigh the minimum salary that you would have to pay, then consider other alternatives to hiring a permanent employee. You may want to hire someone for 10 to 20 hours a week until the business reaches a point where full-time employees are required.

There are many staffing options available and each has its pros and cons. Full-time employees work a set number of hours on a standard salary. Having someone around full-time can provide peace of mind, knowing someone is minding the shop when you can't be there. Part-time employees offer flexibility in scheduling and cost less, but you may spend extra time in training and, if they have jobs elsewhere, worker loyalty may be compromised. Temporary employees may be useful for the short-term projects such as the busy holiday selling season.

Says Tom Algie, owner of Practically Everything in Settle:

I took on three members of staff after 18 months. I had moved to bigger premises and started opening for seven days instead of five. Two of them were absolutely brilliant and are still with me, but the third one didn't work out. I now have another two and they are all great. I advertised to begin with and then found the others by word of mouth. My advice would be to definitely ask for references. I gave all my staff proper job descriptions and they have a free hand to run the shop when I am not there.

It is important to have regular and open communication with your staff. Any staff members who can react effectively to problematic or antagonistic customers or suppliers are worth nurturing. Additionally, those who work under their own initiative and are eager to take on more responsibility can be a valuable asset to your business. If they are dependable, reliable and trustworthy your business can be taken to new heights.

EMPLOYMENT REGULATIONS

If you intend to employ people, you need to comply with a number of regulations. Any owner of a business quickly discovers that there are many laws and potential legal pitfalls in relation to employing staff. Employers need to keep themselves up to date as new obligations and regulations are introduced frequently.

A well-drafted contract of employment geared to the particular role of the individual employee is crucial to protecting your business interests and to reducing the potential for dispute. In addition, clearly drafted policies and procedures on specific areas such as sickness absence, handling of grievance and disciplinary issues, health and safety, equal opportunities and so on will really help you if you are faced with these situations.

As soon as you take someone on, you should draw up a contract of employment as this will prevent any disputes arising. By law (Employment Rights Act), all employees are entitled to receive a written statement of employment from their employer within two months of starting work. Written particulars have to be included to break down or explain in detail the terms and conditions of employment and by law you are required to provide these details to your employee. The following details should be included.

- ☐ Names of employer and employee.
- ☐ Date the employment started.
- ☐ Job title and a brief description of main duties.
- ☐ Address where employee will be working.
- ☐ Scale or rate of pay.
- ☐ At what intervals employee will be paid (weekly, monthly).
- ☐ Employee's working hours.
- ☐ Employee's holiday entitlement.
- ☐ Terms relating to injury, sickness and sick pay.
- ☐ Period of employment.
- ☐ Pension details.
- ☐ Disciplinary and grievance procedures.
- ☐ If the job is full-time, part-time, temporary or contractual.
- ☐ Length of notice.
- ☐ A clause allowing you to end the contract after a trial period.
- ☐ Collective agreements (trade unions).

You can get advice about drawing up a written contract from Acas (www.acas.org.uk), your solicitor, or a local business support organisation. Free leaflets, published by BIS, are available from your local JobCentre Plus.

Under payroll regulations, all employees must be given itemised pay slips stating any deductions. When taking on an employee, HMRC must be informed. It will set up a PAYE scheme and send you a new employer's starter pack.

Staff and prospective employees must not be discriminated against on the grounds of race, gender, disability, religion, sexual orientation or age.

All employers with five or more staff must offer employees access to a stakeholder pension scheme. You are only exempt from the duty to offer a stakeholder pension if you employ fewer than five staff, or offer an acceptable alternative pension for all your employees. This alternative could be an occupation pension scheme or a grouped personal pension (GPP) scheme that meets the required standards.

Employment regulations include the following.
- ☐ Employment Rights Act 1976.
- ☐ The Maternity and Parental Leave etc Regulations 1999 (as amended).
- ☐ The National Minimum Wage Act 1998.
- ☐ The Working Time Regulations Act 1988 (as amended).
- ☐ The Flexible Working (Procedural Requirements) Regulations 2002.
- ☐ The Employment Act 2002 (and subsequent amendments).
- ☐ Transfer of Undertakings (Protection of Employment) Regulations 2006 (TUPE) – relevant if you have taken on staff through buying a business.

RECRUITMENT

When recruiting staff, look for someone who is enthusiastic, perhaps even excited by the merchandise, caring, helpful, resourceful and knowledgeable about stock. Other characteristics to look for are a positive attitude, a smiling countenance, a creative bent, and a helpful and alert attitude.

There are a number of ways in which you could recruit new employees:

- ☐ advertise locally or in specialised publications;
- ☐ write to colleges and schools for candidates;
- ☐ contact the JobCentre;
- ☐ employment agencies.

JobCentres offer free services, but an employment agency could cost you as much as 20% of the employee's first year's salary. When interviewing, give candidates exact written details of the job description and eventually inform all applicants once you have made a decision.

STAFF RECORDS AND WAGES

Maintaining accurate and up-to-date staff details is a prerequisite in all your dealings with employees. The better you treat your employees, the better they will treat you. Show appreciation for a job well done. You could set targets and give bonuses and always pay wages on time and at competitive rates.

The current national minimum wage is £5.73 an hour, £4.77 for 18 to 21-year-olds, and £3.53 for 16 to 17-year-olds. The wages you pay your staff will depend to some extent on what is the going rate in your area. The Annual Survey of Hours and Earnings (available at www.statistics.gov) carried out by the government gives average weekly wages for a wide range of different types of job. If you have five or more staff, you must provide access to a stakeholder pension scheme. You must deduct tax and National Insurance contributions from your employees' wages and pay these to HMRC.

It is a criminal offence to employ anyone, full or part-time, aged 16 or over, who does not have leave to enter or remain in the UK and/or who is not entitled to work in the UK. There are 13 types of documents that are acceptable as proof of entitlement. They include a documented P45, a P60, a birth certificate issued within the UK or the Republic of Ireland, a work permit or a British passport showing the holder has right of abode or re-admission to the UK. Protect yourself by asking to see one of them. Temporary National Insurance numbers are not acceptable.

TRAINING STAFF

Linking training and development with your business and investing in your staff is important to success. There are government-sponsored programmes that can help with the training for your business. These are:

- England: www.traintogain.co.uk
- Scotland: www.skillsdevelopmentscotland.co.uk
- Wales: www.learningobservatory.com
- Northern Ireland: www.delni.gov.uk/index/successthroughskills.htm

Having the right people with the right skills is vital to every business and will be recognised by a successful business. Be proactive in training and developing your employees.

5

BUYING AN EXISTING RETAIL BUSINESS

This is a fairly safe option as the risks involved in buying a shop that is already trading are lower than those faced when starting from scratch. Much of the legwork has already been done. There is also a recognised customer base you should be able to retain, and a lot known about the shop's turnover and profit, as well as what stock to keep. Buying an established business means that the shop layout and design is in place and you can start generating income immediately.

The disadvantage, however, is that the business may be rundown or financially struggling and could require a lot of development work and financial investment. Professional fees for solicitors and accountants arising from the purchase may be considerable. The seller may also want you to buy existing stock which may not suit your taste, and honour previous agreements, contracts and arrangements entered into by them. The business may have alienated customers and if you are not made aware of this it would be difficult to turn it around even with an 'Under New Management' sign.

The price of the shop will depend on where the business is located, the quality of its fixtures and fittings, how successful it is and whether you are buying a freehold or a leasehold business. A freehold will include the value of the building and the commercial value of the business and its fixtures and fittings. A leasehold means paying for the business, fixtures and fittings, goodwill and the right to occupy the premises for the length of the lease.

Check the state of the premises, fittings and equipment and decide whether you will have to spend money on refurbishing or replacing assets. Consider the condition and value of the stock you are buying and that all retail products are within their sell-by dates.

You will need a survey to be sure you know the value of the property. A full structural survey tells you about most aspects of the property, including plumbing and electricity. Valuations are a necessary expense. You can save yourself a lot of money by obtaining accurate information from them.

Ask an accountant to advise you on the seller's accounts so that you can evaluate the business and the price that is being asked. The accounts should show:

☐ expenditure – professional fees, rates, heating and lighting, telephone and stationery, repairs and renewals, wages, advertising and promotions, miscellaneous;
☐ income – sales.

If you decide to buy, register your interest in buying the shop with the professional adviser who is normally employed by the owners to sell up. Ensure there are no problems with the business and complete a preliminary due diligence before you make a firm offer. Evaluate any key risks that may be associated with future trading.

If you are still interested, obtain professional advice to help you value the business. Choose advisers with appropriate experience who can also assist in analysing historical information and trends. Calculate your initial offer and your maximum offer and then submit it. Set out the payment structure and complete legal due diligence. As soon as the deal is completed announce the change of ownership in a positive way.

To find shops for sale, look in your local newspapers or associated magazines. Daltons Business, the businesses for sale website (www.daltonsbusiness.com) that is part of *Daltons Weekly*, advertises a range of shops for sale. Business transfer agents and estate agents concerned with retail businesses can also be helpful. Your local authority may also keep a register of commercial property. In addition, check out the following online business sellers:

- ☐ www.nationwidebusinesses.co.uk
- ☐ www.businessesforsale.com
- ☐ www.business-sale.com

TIP

- ☐ Use the advice and experience of a business broker.
- ☐ Don't negotiate anything before it is due.
- ☐ If you make an offer, make sure you like it.
- ☐ Walk away if you made a fair offer and negotiations are not looking good.
- ☐ Get help on any part of the process you are not sure about.
- ☐ Don't make any offers you are not ready to make good on.

Questions to ask

Consider the following questions before choosing a shop to buy.

- ☐ Do you want to live in a town or in a rural area?
- ☐ Do you need living accommodation above the shop?
- ☐ Why is the business for sale?
- ☐ Is it suffering from too many competitors?
- ☐ Are there cash flow problems?
- ☐ Does the shop present an opportunity for growth?
- ☐ Do the premises need decorating or refitting?
- ☐ What is included in the sale?
- ☐ Are there any maintenance costs?
- ☐ Will any staff need training?
- ☐ What are terms and conditions of the lease?
- ☐ When is the rent reviewed?

☐ Are there reliable suppliers?
☐ Is the shop really worth the asking price?
☐ Does it have any debts?
☐ What is the value of the stock?
☐ How much is there?
☐ What sells quickly and what is slow moving?
☐ Does the range meet the needs of the customers?
☐ Which products are the most profitable?
☐ Has there been consistent profit over the years?
☐ Is there a seasonal cash flow?
☐ Is the owner seeking goodwill?
☐ Are the accounts available for examination?
☐ Are there accounts showing the current position?

Examples of shops for sale

Successful Cycle and Canoe Shop for sale
Highlands of Scotland
Price: £40,000
Turnover: £200,000 to £500,00
Profit: £100,000

Independent Bookshop
North Yorkshire
Price: £175,000
Turnover: £500,000
Profit: £100,000

Desirable Florist
West Sussex
Price: £70,000
Turnover: £245,000
Profit undisclosed

Says Tom Algie of Practically Everything in Settle:

❮ It was Christmas Eve and I had agreed a redundancy package with my employers at the Settle-Carlisle Railway Development Company. I was due to leave at the end of January with no job to go to. A small local shop (the Toolbox) in Settle was closing down and had a closing down sale, 33% off everything. I had just turned 40 and knew I liked the shop.

I bought a few things then went back in and asked the owner if he had tried selling the shop and why he was closing. He said he had tried but he had only been trading for eight months and wanted to go back to the building trade. He rented the premises off the landlord next door for £80 a week. I offered to buy all the stock in the shop if I could agree terms with the landlord, which I subsequently did, ten minutes later. I said I would have the £5,000 in cash on Boxing Day. He shut the shop and when I next saw him he gave me supplier details and showed me how to operate the till. I opened on Boxing Day. My son Joe helped me for one to two days a week initially, which was very useful.

Buying a franchise

This is a great way to start your own business. It allows you to skip much of the legwork of starting a shop from scratch. There are many pluses involved in taking on a franchise, as well as a few risks and cautions. The greatest benefit of taking over an existing franchise is that it is already in operation and has a solid customer base.

Before you enter into a franchise agreement, ask existing franchisees and customers about the business, attend franchising exhibitions and assess the reputation of the franchisor. Most franchises will be based on a sound, healthy business and profit model but check for sustainability. A franchisor establishes the content of the business, the type of goods, services and price, performing standards, design and plan of premises, initial training and outgoing support and training.

It is generally considered that successful franchise operations have a much lower failure rate than completely new businesses. You will also have a realistic snapshot of past profitability. However, don't purchase an existing franchise with expectations of an immediately booming business. First, study market trends and forecasts.

A franchise is the legal arrangement where the franchisor gives permission for the franchisee to use its name, brand, product, trademark, operation and service in return for payment. Franchised businesses are more likely to succeed than many other start-ups because they have a proven track record as well as established and effective processes in place.

ADVANTAGES OF FRANCHISING

- ☐ Market knowledge.
- ☐ Innovation.
- ☐ Access to a successful business formula.
- ☐ A national advertising campaign and recognised brand name.
- ☐ Support and training programmes in sales and all business skills.
- ☐ Help with securing funding for your investment, as well as discounted bulk-buy supplies for outlets when you are in operation.

DRAWBACKS OF FRANCHISING

- ☐ Cost may be too high – you pay an initial fee (often between £5,000 to £10,000, but as much as £250,000) to buy into a franchise.
- ☐ Paying an ongoing royalty on sales whether you are making a profit or not.
- ☐ No flexibility.

□ Risks that are beyond your control.
□ The franchise doesn't deliver.

BEING PART OF A LARGER ORGANISATION

According to the British Franchise Association (BFA, www.thebfa.org), customers will understand that you will be offering the best possible value for money and service and that although you run your own show you are part of a much larger organisation.

Each business outlet is owned and operated by the franchisee. However, the franchisor retains control over the way in which products and services are marketed and sold, and controls the quality and standards of the business.

The franchisor will receive an initial fee from the franchisee, payable at the outset, together with on-going management service fees, usually based on a percentage of annual turnover or mark-ups on supplies. In return, the franchisor has an obligation to support the franchise network, notably with training, product development, advertising, promotional activities and with a specialist range of management services.

To further understand the franchising scenario:

□ speak to current franchisees;

□ visit a franchise exhibition – there are major annual franchise exhibitions in Birmingham, London, Manchester and Dublin;

□ read the trade and national press – trade publications include *Business Franchise* (www.businessfranchise.com), *The Franchise Magazine* (www.thefranchisemagazine.-net) and *Franchise World* (www.franchiseworld.co.uk);

□ get information from the BFA – order the information pack online (www.thebfa.org). The BFA also holds regular one-day franchisee workshops at various locations across the country. At these workshops you can learn more from franchisees, franchisors, banking and legal professionals. The course will enable you to assess whether franchising is right for you. Attendance costs £75, plus VAT. Further information on these seminars is available from the Help and Advice page of the BFA website. There are also a number of interesting franchising books on the market and guides from the BFA, as well as the Franchise Survey, which provides a detailed in-depth analysis of franchising in the UK.

Ensure the franchisor provides the following particulars:

□ Locations being offered.
□ Competitors.
□ Details about themselves, history and success rates.
□ Type of support and training.
□ All the costs, including up-front fee and royalties.

☐ Projected financial returns.

☐ Terms of agreement.

Franchise opportunities are available through:

☐ Franchise UK, Unit 67, Station Road, Hailsham, East Sussex BN27 2ET, tel: 0800 019 9662, www.franchise-uk.co.uk

☐ Select your Franchise, Fryern House, 125 Winchester Road, Chandlers Ford, Hampshire SO53 2DR, tel: 0870 760 1199, email: md@selectyourfranchise.co, www.selectyourfranchise.com/uk/

☐ whichfranchise.com, 375 West George Street, Glasgow G2 4LW, tel: 0141 204 0050, email: enquiry@whichfranchise.com, www.whichfranchise.com

☐ The UK Franchise Directory, Franchise House, 56 Surrey Street, Norwich NR1 3FD, tel: 01603 620301, www.thefranchisedirectory.net

Further advice and information can be obtained from the British Franchise Association (BFA, www.thebfa.org) and Franchise Development Services (FDS, www.fdsfranchise.com).

6
RECORD-KEEPING AND TAXES

Taxation represents a significant proportion of small business expenditure. It has been reported that small businesses allot about 16% of their outgoings on tax obligations, making it their third biggest expense. There are laws governing how various taxes are calculated, when they are to be paid and what happens if you do not meet your obligations.

HMRC viewing powers

In the past, HM Revenue & Customs (HMRC) had powers to inspect your records and documents as an enquiry went along. Under new rules the taxman will now be able to ask you for things entirely separately from any investigation of a specific tax return. In addition, HMRC will be able to get information from someone other than you as the taxpayer. However, any approach to the third party must be with your agreement or formally sanctioned by higher authorities within HMRC.

These compliance checks (also known as enquiries, visits and inspections) could entail looking at your PAYE records, purchase receipts and your till roll, as well as your bank statements. HMRC have to be able to visit business premises and check on the tax liabilities that involve things such as valuing stock on hand or checking your books for VAT purposes. A key safeguard throughout these powers is that they have to be used 'reasonably'.

Under these rules, HMRC will no longer have to wait for your tax return to be submitted before asking questions about issues that it covers. That form of power is already available to them in the context of VAT; however, it will now start to apply for income tax, capital gains tax and corporation tax. This means that HMRC will be able to ask to see the books of the business during the year rather than waiting until after the year end.

Keeping accurate records

Keeping accurate records of your business's accounting activities is vital. Don't get buried in a quagmire of bills, invoices and tax demands. As well as giving you an idea of how well your business is doing, without proper records you could end up paying the wrong amount of tax.

You must register with the HMRC within the first three months, even if you already use a self-assessment tax return. There are penalties for not registering.

For the very smallest business, the absolute minimum accounting records would include:

□ bank statements, cheque books and paying-in books;
□ original invoices for all purchases and copy invoices for sales;

□ PAYE records, even if the only employees are directors;
□ VAT records if you are registered, including reconciliations for the amounts paid;
□ stock at year end;
□ fixed assets.

You should also consider keeping:

□ a cash book – keeps track of all your financial incomings and outgoings;
□ a sales ledger – records any invoices you may have sent out;
□ a purchase ledger – records money you owe other companies;
□ a petty cash book – keeps account of all miscellaneous spending.

When dealing with cash, you will need till receipts and a record book to keep track of it all. Try and keep records of your pricing policy as this will affect the overall gross profit rate of your business. HMRC will look at your trading results to see if your gross profit is in line with industry norms.

Your responsibilities

You are responsible for the entries you make on your tax return, and if HMRC have any queries you will need to go back to your records. Bank statements, receipts and cash transaction records are all essential for working out your profits for the year and HMRC use this information to calculate your tax and National Insurance.

TAX

The tax year runs from 6 April to 5 April. Tax is due in two equal instalments: on 31 January (during that tax year) and 31 July (after the end of the tax year). These interim payments are based on the previous year's tax liability. A balancing payment is due on the following 31 January, to adjust the difference between the amounts paid and the tax due as a result of actual profits.

NATIONAL INSURANCE

National Insurance (NI) is a contribution towards state benefits, such as retirement pension, unemployment and incapacity benefits. If you employ staff you must make sure that employers' and employees' NI contributions are paid.

There are four different types of NI.

□ Class 1 NICs – payable by anyone who is employed. They are a percentage of your earnings above a certain threshold. Employers deduct Class 1 NICs automatically, along with PAYE income tax.

□ Class 2 NICs – payable by anyone who is self-employed. It is a fixed weekly amount, paid by direct debit or quarterly bill. If earnings are below £4,635 a year, you may be entitled to an exemption or refund.

☐ Class 3 NICs – these are voluntary payments. They cover shortfalls in your NI contribution record and help protect your entitlement to state pension and bereavement benefits.

☐ Class 4 NICs – payable by self-employed people. They are currently 8% of your annual taxable profit from self-employment, but you only start paying Class 4 when your profits reach a certain amount (between £5,225 and £34,840). You include Class 4 on your tax return.

National Insurance for your business type

Sole trader

This means that you are an individual who is self-employed. There are two types of NI for the self-employed: Class 2 and Class 4. The self-employed pay less NI than employees, but they receive significantly fewer benefits. VAT is payable if you reach the registration threshold.

Partnership

Each partner pays income tax, through the Self Assessment system, as well as Class 2 and Class 4 NI. The business itself also pays VAT once you reach the registration threshold.

Limited company

If you set up a limited company (and are therefore an employee), you pay tax on your income every time you are paid. This is called PAYE (Pay As You Earn). You have to deduct tax and NICs from your salary through your company's payroll, which you have to set up. Your business also has to pay employer's NICs for its employees. Company directors need to file statutory documents, such as accounts and annual returns.

CORPORATION TAX

There is also corporation tax to think about, which is charged on company profits. Companies have to calculate their own corporation tax and then make a payment to HMRC. A tax rate of 21% applies to small businesses with a taxable profit of up to £300,000. Companies with profits of more than £1.5m pay corporation tax in quarterly instalments, while other companies pay nine months after the accounting year end.

Profits and expenses

When you are calculating profits, remember HMRC has strict rules on what can be counted as a business expense. Allowable expenses include rent and running costs for premises, the cost of goods bought as stock and then resold, financing and marketing costs. Costs that are not allowed include personal expenses (travel to work), living expenses or clothes, money spent entertaining clients, and fines (for example, parking tickets).

When working out your profits, you cannot count the cost of purchasing premises and equipment as an expense. You claim capital allowance on these, which allows you to deduct a proportion of the cost from your taxable profit over several years. The allowance is calculated as a fixed percentage of an item's value each year. Capital allowances range from 4% to 100%, depending on your type of business and what you are buying.

Capital gains tax (CGT) is a tax on a successful investment (property, shares or sale of a business). If you sell something for more than you paid for it, CGT might be payable. CGT will not usually be payable on the sale of your home (although you could end up paying some if you claim some of your mortgage payments as a business expense). Limited companies pay corporation tax on capital gains because these are treated as part of the company's taxable profit. Self-employed people pay CGT at their top rate of income tax. There are allowances and exemptions.

Provided you have informed HMRC that you have started your business, you can claim expenses incurred before you started trading as allowable expenses in your first year. There are exceptions, such as training courses and the cost of forming a limited company. Solicitors or accountants will be able to offer advice on all of this.

Records must be kept for six years. Your accountant will be able to give you advice on how best to keep records. You might decide to go for a computerised system, which will help your accountant to draw up your accounts at the end of the year. Bookkeeping is not just a means of satisfying the tax department; it can tell you how well your business is performing, how you could cut costs, and which of your customers are buying from you the most. Neglecting it means your accountant will take longer to draw up your accounts and in the long run will cost you more money.

Any HMRC office will be able to let you have a copy of *Self assessment: A general guide to keeping records* or a leaflet on corporation tax.

Value Added Tax (VAT) explained

VAT is a transaction tax on sales of goods and services. If your business sells products or services at a total value worth more than the amount set by the government, VAT registration is compulsory. This threshold is currently £68,000.

The VAT you charge (currently 15% but will return to 17.5% in 2010) on the goods you sell, is known as output tax. You will be able to reclaim any VAT you pay on goods and services purchased for your business. This is input tax. It is the difference between the two (output tax minus input tax) that you pay to HMRC. It is normally collected four times a year. However, if you paid more VAT than you have charged, you will be due a refund.

Fines for late payment or procedural failures can be severe. If need be, seek advice from an accountant. HMRC also produces a wide range of helpful information, including 'Should I be registered for VAT?' You can also download other useful forms and publications.

ALTERNATIVE FLAT RATE SCHEME

You might be interested in an optional flat rate scheme (FRS) for eligible small businesses. Under this scheme you continue to issue tax invoices to VAT registered customers, but the

VAT payable every quarter is calculated as a percentage of your VAT-inclusive turnover. You apply the appropriate flat rate percentage for your type of business. This scheme cannot be used with the retail schemes or the cash accounting scheme. Full details of the FRS can be found in 'Notice 700/1 Flat Rate Scheme for small businesses'. It will help you to decide whether or not the scheme is suitable for you.

With effect from April 2009, the test that requires a business to check that its total income is less than £187,500 for entry into the VAT Flat Rate Scheme has been removed. Instead, eligibility to join the scheme is determined solely by the taxable turnover of the business, which must be less that £150,000.

Selecting professional advisers

Good advisers, usually an accountant and a solicitor, are vital when dealing with complex business issues. If you choose poorly you may find that your business suffers because someone is not keeping you properly informed. An accountant should be recruited during the planning phase.

Receiving advice from the start can prevent problems in the future. Accountancy firms offer a wide range of business services, including what form the business should take, bookkeeping, drawing up the annual accounts, preparing tax and VAT returns, handling the operation of PAYE, giving tax and business advice and so on.

FINDING AN ACCOUNTANT

Here are some ways to identify the right accountant.

☐ Ask business friends and colleagues.
☐ Through your bank manager or solicitor.
☐ Contact your local business support organisation, Chamber of Commerce or Business Link.
☐ Look in the local papers and trade magazines.
☐ Look in the *Yellow Pages* and *Thomson Local* directories.
☐ Use the website Search Accountant (www.searchaccountant.co.uk) which includes a directory of UK accountants.

There are also several organisations that regulate the accountancy profession. Members of these organisations are professionally qualified and are bound to uphold the business ethics their organisations maintain. They are:

☐ The Institute of Chartered Accountants in England and Wales (ICAEW), www.icaew.co.uk
☐ The Association of Chartered Accountants (ACCA), www.accaglobal.com
☐ The Institute of Chartered Accounts of Scotland (ICAS), www.icas.org.uk

Prepare a shortlist with a minimum of two and a maximum of six practices that you want to call. Ask them for information about size, specialisation and experience. Basically, you want an accountant who specialises in small business work. Request an informal first meeting with no charge.

Before committing yourself, check on the estimated fees and billing arrangements. You should not be afraid to question and negotiate fees. Quite often the first-year fees are competitively low and then increase steeply in the second year. Some firms will want you to pay on a monthly basis, others may do the work and then bill you when accounts are produced. One alternative is to use the free advice offered by your local support agency.

FINDING A SOLICITOR

A solicitor can advise on general issues. There are different areas of law and solicitors who specialise in them. The Law Society operates a scheme called Lawyers for Your Business (LFYB), a network of 1,200 legal firms offering specialist advice to small and medium-sized businesses. Solicitors will give an initial free consultation when you are starting up, running or growing your business. Thereafter, ask for an estimate of costs or a daily rate.

A directory of legal firms and individual solicitors that are affiliated to the Law Society can be found at www.solicitors-online.com and can be searched by name, specialisation and area. Solicitors UK (www.solicitors-uk.org.uk) has a directory of UK solicitors and at Lawyer Locator (www.lawyerlocator.co.uk) you can find a local solicitor or law firm in your area. As well as using an online directory service, recommendations from other companies or business associates, such as your bank manager or accountant, are a good way to start.

7
SETTING UP SHOP

Many people think of shopping as a relaxing leisure activity and, while you may have an eager audience willing to buy, you need to win the attention of potential customers. How you present your shop is extremely important in creating an environment that is conducive to shopping. One way to do this is to use interchangeable, captivating display systems to keep your shop interesting, appealing and fresh.

Shop interiors

Choose displays and fixtures that are suited to your target market. In the 1970s, the philosophy was 'pile it high, sell it cheap' but today a retailer needs to use more contemporary and sophisticated retail fixtures to attract and keep customers satisfied. You need to design a space that makes it easy for your customers by using retail displays that allow and encourage customers to keep browsing and shopping. A customer-friendly, easy navigation path will lead your customers through all your products. In addition, an average person's field of vision is around 170 degrees so keep that in mind when designing your retail space.

There are a number of basic retail floor plans: straight (for most types of shops), diagonal (self-service types), angular (high-end specialty), geometric (clothing and apparel) and mixed (incorporating straight, diagonal and angular).

When you have bought your display fixtures, props, shelves, racks and showcases, estimate how many square feet are required for each category of merchandise. List all the categories you intend stocking and then break them down into sub-categories, then into individual sizes and styles. Once you have done this, you can calculate each sub-category as a percentage of the overall category and each category as a percentage of your entire stock.

Eventually you can decide where to place your merchandise. You will need to work out what needs to be placed on shelves, racks and display props. Some may need shelves and racks, others showcases, some hanging space only. Obviously, all of this will depend on the type of products you intend selling. Remember that moving and changing displays and merchandise will keep your shop compelling to the customer. The look and feel of your colour scheme should reflect your personality and the personality and theme of the shop.

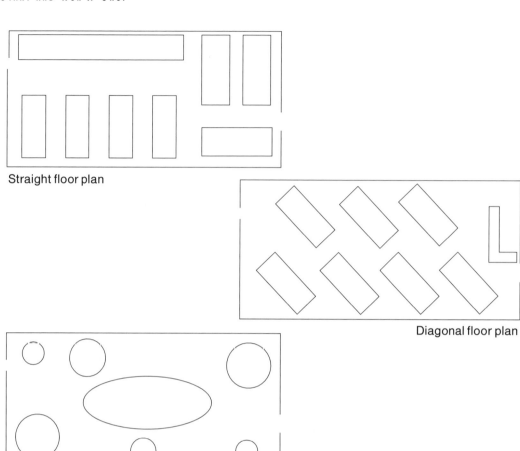

Straight floor plan

Diagonal floor plan

Angular floor plan

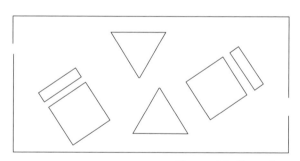

Geometric floor plan

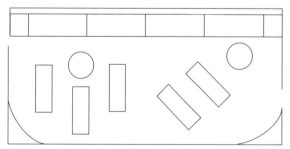

Mixed floor plan

Shop exteriors

Look for a shop front that has one or more windows. A shop window is one of the proven forms of advertising and if you create an attractive product display it can draw customers in. Take time to plan your window. To design an effective visual display, consider balance, size of objects, colour, focal point, lighting and simplicity. Interior and exterior décor, merchandise display, shop windows and ambience are all inextricably linked.

The outside of your shop should be eye-catching and welcoming. Planning permission may be required if you intend altering the exterior of a building, doing extensions or erecting billboard advertisements. You will need to apply to the planning department of your local authority outlining what you propose to do. There are also local building regulations governing the way building work may be carried out.

Legislation covering shop exteriors is a large subject and differs from council to council. For instance, in Cambridge with its large concentration of listed buildings any alterations to these structures, whether internal or external, could be subject to listed building consent. Guidance should be sought from the local planning authority.

Communities and Local Government (www.communities.gov.uk/corporate/) publishes a handbook called *Outdoor Advertisements and Signs: A Guide for Advertisers*, which provides the planning regulations for alterations to all types of shop exteriors and signage. This provides owners with the information to determine if any changes to their shop front or installation of any signs will need a planning application.

In Cambridge, the council has produced a shop front design guide, which is used by planning officers when determining an advertisement consent application. In addition to this, there are Conservation Area appraisals, which should be read if the shop unit falls into one of the city's ten conservation areas.

OUTDOOR ADVERTISEMENTS

If you want to display an outdoor advertisement, the booklet called *Outdoor Advertisements and Signs: A Guide for Advertisers*, prepared by Communities and Local Government (www.communities.gov.uk) is the most comprehensive explanation of how the system of advertisement control works in England. The main section in the booklet explains:

- ☐ how the advertisement control system works;
- ☐ what advertisements are normally permitted;
- ☐ what advertisements need specific permission and how to obtain it;
- ☐ how planning authorities may control the display of advertisements in some special cases.

The advertisement control system consists of rules which are part of the planning control system. The present rule is the Town and Country Planning (Control of Advertisements) Regulations 2007.

Throughout England, local planning authorities are responsible for the day-to-day operation of the advertisement control system, and for deciding whether a particular advertisement should be permitted or not. For this purpose the local planning authority for your area will normally be the district council, the county council or the London borough council if you live in the Greater London area. There are two exceptions to this arrangement.

☐ If your advertisement is to be displayed in any National Park, the planning authority is the National Park authority, or if it is to be displayed within the Broads area then contact the Broads authority.

☐ If your advertisement is to be displayed in an urban development area, the planning authority normally is the Urban Development Corporation for that area.

The control system covers a wide range of advertisements and signs including:

☐ posters and notices;
☐ placards and boards;
☐ fascia signs and protecting signs;
☐ pole signs and canopy signs;
☐ models and devices;
☐ advance signs and directional signs;
☐ estate agents' boards;
☐ captive balloon advertising;
☐ flag advertisements;
☐ price markets and price displays.

LISTED BUILDINGS

If your premises have Listed Building status, you will need to check what you are able to change or not change. Contact the Department of Culture (www.culture.gov.uk) for advice.

Getting the most out of your shop

SHOP AND DISPLAY EQUIPMENT ASSOCIATION (SDEA)

The Shop and Display Equipment Association (www.shopdisplay.org) advises independents on how to make the most of their store environments to help drive sales. Their top tips for retail success areas follows.

☐ Strip out the clutter to create a clean and more spacious environment. For a truly unique look, add a feature. This format works equally well for a local convenience store or boutique.

☐ Branding is vital – the look of a store must reinforce the overall corporate identity, even if you are an independent. Ensure your store stands out from the crowd.

- Consider the items that you stock and how they fit together, their colours and styles, what they say and what you want to say to the public.

- Identify your target market and aim your product displays and shopfittings at that audience.

- Choose a relevant theme and enlarge on it – make it the very essence of your shop.

- The window and in-store displays must work together to entice the customer in and excite them into purchasing. This can be done with good display props and accessories.

- Create a stunning window display to pull the shoppers in. Be creative, use lots of colour and have fun. When the shop is closed, the window display continues to work for you so it needs to be powerful.

- Another popular alternative is to open up the entire storefront so that the customer can see right through the store.

- Large format graphics can also be used in place of traditional props and are a great way to convey a corporate 'lifestyle' if you have more than one store.

- The shopfittings and display equipment, while smart and modern, should also embody the store's outlook and allow the products to shine. They should be relatively neutral, unless of course you want to enlarge on a corporate look. The design, innovation and creation of unique display systems and props, the use of cutting edge materials to manufacture traditional systems, or the creation of new systems from a material normally associated with another application, can all make a difference.

- For the perfect retail mix, add a variety of in-store events, special offers and customer loyalty benefits to ensure additional footfall and sales in quiet times.

SDEA has an array of suppliers and manufacturers who can offer you innovative products and services. Many will be able to put together a themed project, as well as designing, manufacturing and installing it for you. The SDEA Directory (priced at £10) lists all their members with detailed descriptions. The showcase gallery offers a visual interpretation of their display items and quick reference guides help you locate a supplier by the retail trade or the products they specialise in.

OTHER SHOPFITTERS

Team Design Shopfitting (www.nfrnonline.com) is a national association of independent store design and shopfitting companies offering a complete planning and shopfitting service throughout the UK. Says David Batcock of Team Design Sales:

All our refurbishments are individually planned. The designer's experience and local knowledge is used to create layouts that produce improved traffic flow around the shop, attractive displays and more efficient use of space. This in turn generates greater sales and increased profits for the retailer.

During the initial assessment of the shop's potential, particular attention is given to planning the product range, including looking carefully at items that are performing well and need additional displays, as well as those that need to be reduced or eliminated. In this way, the correct equipment for the products can be installed and an effective layout produced.

By using multi-tiered 'waterfall' shelving to display magazines, it is possible to have a nine-shelf display where only five ordinary shelves existed before, therefore creating a massive increase in display area while utilising the same floor space. The same principle applies to our 21-tier card unit.

Naturally, a full re-fit can involve considerable financial outlay, but it is expected that this sum would be recouped over a period of time, due to the increased sales attracted by the refurbishment. However, many retailers delay the necessary refurbishment of their shops because of worries about costs. In fact, it is not always necessary to undertake a complete refurbishment. We are happy to discuss partial re-fits with retailers. In this way, a shop can be refurbished in stages, over a planned period of time.

New card and card/wrap units will improve a shop's image at very little cost. Many retailers will also be surprised at how cost-effective modern counters are. Specifically designed and built to suit the individual outlet, in order to provide the necessary space for computers, tills and lottery terminals, such counters immediately create a more professional image in a shop. We are also Post Office recommended suppliers of open-plan counters to independent retailers.

The introduction of a colour theme is another easy way to enhance the interior. Coloured trimmings on card units and counters can be echoed by matching coloured ticket insert and re-painting walls and doors. The addition of coloured skirting on modular shelving, window graphics and in-store commodity-group graphics in complementary styles creates a coordinated look throughout the shop.

Once a layout has been agreed, Team Design Shopfitting's personnel will organise a schedule for the work. In order to comply with current health and safety requirements, it is increasingly necessary to recommend that shops are closed for all or part of a re-fit. Where it is necessary for a shop to remain open (such as a Post Office) a temporary counter can be set up and areas of the shop barriered off. A refurbishment will usually take longer when a shop remains open. Lost sales are soon retrieved by additional local publicity and a high profile shop re-opening after the work has been completed.

Listening to music

If you plan to play background music in your premises you will need to obtain licences from the Performing Rights Society (PRS), known as PRS for Music (www.prsformusic.com), and Phonographic Performance Limited (PPL, www.ppluk.com). There is an annual fee for these licences. There are more than 40 tariffs, which depend on the type and size of the premises and the nature and extent to which the music is used. For example, an audible area of up to 100 square metres (1,076 square feet) is charged £136.70 for background and demonstration music by PRS for Music. These tariff rates are agreed with national trade associations and representative bodies.

8
RUNNING YOUR SHOP

Right product, right price, right time

A successful retail business depends considerably on offering the right product, at the right price, at the right time. Therefore, it is paramount that you locate the best sources for the products or product lines you intend selling. Merchandise can be bought from wholesalers, manufacturers, importers, attending trade shows or buyer's markets, auctions, online and by joining buying groups. Before you buy, try to visit a competitor or a store selling a product line similar to what you plan to sell. Browse the shop's product selection and note which products seem to be selling well and which items are in the clearance bin.

Once you have located several sources, evaluate each supplier on quality products, delivery and customer service. This information can be gathered through references, marketing material or by asking the sales representative how they conduct business. Also consider price, shipping, terms of sale, return merchandise and stability. Keep your product offering simple in the beginning. Learning to pick a hot product before it becomes hot is a skill that comes from knowing your market but as soon as you have a hot selling item, re-order quickly. As your business grows, so can your product line.

Says Amanda Hartley of Amanda's Blue Orchid Florist in Hull:

> *I do try and keep up with the trends, such as the latest wrappings and styles, but my customer base is happy with what I do. I call it modern – something between funky and traditional. I have my own unique style that you can spot a mile off in a city where every shop seems to send out practically the same thing.*
>
> *However, trends in the business are a different matter. If I were to show you my business plan and show you around my shop, you would think you were in the wrong place. It has gone a different way to what I had planned (pretty flowers, pretty cards, pretty teddies) to stunning flowers, angel ornaments and fascinators. You have to sell what people want, when they want it. It also helps to only stock what you would buy yourself. If you don't like it, don't stock it.*

Fake goods

Recent research has found that nearly a quarter of all small and medium-sized enterprises were affected by counterfeiting, creating one of the biggest problems for businesses of all kinds around the world. Intellectual property (IP) crimes have spread from small industries producing poor quality, counterfeit fashion accessories and goods to massive manufacturing plants that can produce cheap copies of everything from electrical appliances to medicines.

A new best practice toolkit has been launched which gives businesses practical advice on how they can better protect themselves from the dangers of fake goods entering business supply chains. The Supply Chain Toolkit has been produced by the Intellectual Property Office's (www.ipo.gov.uk) IP Crime Group. It includes a step-by-step approach on what action should be taken if counterfeits are found within the supply chain and guidance on how to strengthen and protect IP assets. Tens of billions of pounds worth of counterfeit goods are seized across national borders each year.

Establishing your pricing

The best selling products will never earn any real money if your margin is too small. Choose products with recurring sales value. When you look at the price of the product, don't forget to calculate the direct and indirect costs (such as overheads) of selling your goods. Your aim should be to set your prices at the level that gives you the highest profits possible.

You need to know what customers will pay, what competitors charge and the cost of each product. There is no clear-cut or agreed way of establishing prices for products. You could use the level of costs as a way of fixing price but others argue that the price should be set by what the market can bear. The internet also plays a part, since people can go online and order from almost any location. Therefore, you will need to price your merchandise based on the internet as well.

It's probably best to think in terms of a range of prices. The lowest price you set should be fixed by the cost; you shouldn't go below this price. You may decide to go for prestige pricing, which means pricing your products to appeal to those of your potential customers with the highest incomes, or those seeking the snob value of buying a high-priced item. Although this may mean bigger profits, it could also attract competitors offering lower prices.

Alternatively, you may go for backward pricing, where customers dictate the price they will pay. You then have to work backwards to tailor what can be provided at that price, making sure all costs and profit margins are included. Price breaks can also be useful. For some products, it is better to break prices at 99p rather than round them up to the pound. Remember that cutting prices is not normally a good idea for any business.

PRICE SETTING

According to the Small Business Advice Service (SBAS), price setting can be separated into five different stages.

☐ Household and personal overheads per year: food, clothes, mortgage, holidays, lighting, heating, rates, telephone, tax and national insurance.

☐ Business overheads and costs per year: your salary (household and personal overheads), rent and rates, heating and lighting, wages, advertising, stationery, interest on bank loan or overdraft, materials, other expenses (such as legal and accounting fees).

☐ The estimated number of sales during the period: cost per item = business overhead ÷ estimated sales.

☐ The profit you would like (say, 50% of cost): profit per item = cost per item $\times$ 50 ÷ 100.

☐ The price per item therefore = cost per item + profit.

Your gross margin equals the sale price less the cost of the item. Below is a chart showing what mark-up gives what gross margin on an item costing £5:

Mark-up %	Sale price	Gross margin	Gross margin %
100	£10.00	£5.00	50
50	£7.50	£2.50	33
33	£6.65	£1.65	25
25	£6.25	£1.25	20

Return policy

You should establish a return policy, which should be posted near the cash register as well as stated plainly on all receipts. Typically a return policy states the number of days within which a customer can return an item, and whether the store will refund in cash or store credit. Many shops have very liberal return policies because they believe it is essential to good customer service and repeat business.

In retailing, there is a mark-up on the high side as well as on the low side of a given formula. The high side is fine if quality is of the highest calibre, but don't be greedy. Even if customers love the merchandise, they often won't pay the price. Rather, opt for fair pricing which allows you to build a good reputation and can guarantee return customers. A practical approach can be based on the function of supply and demand. Luxury items and hand-crafted merchandise generally allow for higher mark-ups, while your basic and essential products may have a smaller profit margin. Retail mark-up typically runs between 30% and 40%. If you plan to sell a £19.95 item to your customers. That item will probably cost between £14 and £15 wholesale.

Special offers and discounts

Loyalty schemes have been around for some time. Most operate on a system of discounts, vouchers or gifts for points accumulated. The proliferation of these schemes could produce loyalty fatigue among customers, so it might be a good idea to go back to simple discounting and 'everyday low prices'.

However, a simple loyalty scheme can be set up very quickly and easily. The Oxford Institute of Retail Management identifies five basic kinds of loyalty.

☐ Monopoly loyalty – where there is often no choice available (such as in rural areas).
☐ Inertial loyalty – where consumers do not actively seek an alternative.
☐ Price loyalty – where consumers evaluate alternatives on the basis of price alone.
☐ Incentivised loyalty – where points mean prizes.
☐ Emotional loyalty – where image, choice and customer satisfaction dominates.

When discounting, the volume of sales required to ensure the same level of profit can often be much higher than realised. If the trade terms are high, say 50%, then giving a 10% discount to the customer means that sales would only have to increase by 25% in order to make the same profit. However, if the trade terms were only 25%, then sales would have to increase by 66% to make the same profit. Higher discounts to the consumer need to produce greatly increased sales to maintain profit. With an average 40% in trade terms, a discount of 20% would need to produce a doubling in sales to produce the same profit.

Offering credit terms

If your shop offers credit, you are required by the Consumer Credit Act 1974 to be licensed by the Office of Fair Trading (OFT). There are serious penalties for trading with credit without a Consumer Credit Licence. However, you won't need a licence if you are just accepting credit cards or allowing customers to pay their bills in four or fewer instalments within a year beginning on the date of the arrangement.

When considering your application for a licence, the OFT takes into account past conduct, including matters such as personal and business convictions, bankruptcies, customer complaints about the business, as well as likely future problems that might arise through your actions or those of your employees and anyone you are associated with.

You can apply online (www.oft.gov.uk) for a Consumer Credit Licence. It can take two months or longer to get a licence approved. A licence costs about £380, lasts for five years and can be renewed up to one month prior to expiry. If your application is approved, the OFT will send a letter confirming that you are licensed to offer credit, which will include all of the relevant details. You must not use the licence for a business (that is, a business name) or activity that is not stated in the application made or the licence granted.

Now you need to find a finance house through which you can offer credit. Contact your bank, your local Trading Standards Office or your trade association for more information. For more information, contact the Finance & Leasing Association (FLA, www.fla.org.uk) or the Consumer Credit Trade Association (CCTA, www.ccta.co.uk).

Cheque scams

There are a number of cheque scams. It could be a cheque drawn on an account that no longer exists or when the writer knows there are insufficient funds to cover the cheque. You won't know until the cheque has gone through the clearing system and has been returned to your bank. By that time the customer has gone with the goods. You should also look out for forged cheques and stolen chequebooks. For more advice, check www.safefromscams.co.uk

Managing your cash flow

Cash flow is critical to your business survival. It is important, therefore, to monitor your cash flow on a daily basis rather than weekly or monthly. The Department for Business, Innovation and Skills (BIS) believes that proper planning and monitoring of cash flow can help you to spot potential problems. It is important to have a handle on every single cost and every incoming and outgoing in your shop.

Examine your working capital cycle and reconcile the debtors and creditors on your bank statements: decide exactly what payments should be coming in and going out. The Chambers of Commerce cites the following as the five main components of cash flow.

☐ The main inflow of cash is usually the cash from sales. If you sell on credit, your cash inflow is delayed until you are actually paid. Effective credit control is essential. A business that purchases on credit and is paid in cash, such as a retailer, is at a great advantage in cash flow terms.

☐ New finance provides a one-off boost to your cash flow. In the past, most businesses have relied on bank overdraft finance and have reached their borrowing limits quickly. Alternative methods of funding allow you to raise more finances.

☐ The main outflow of cash is the money used for expenditure, including paying for your overheads. Salaries are often the largest and most inflexible cost. Other major costs might include stock, raw materials and any capital expenditure.

☐ VAT and tax are regular cash outflows that tend to be paid out in large lumps. You can be penalised heavily for late payments. Buying significant items just before a VAT period ends, rather than at the start of the next one, can help your cash flow.

☐ Your business needs to give its owners and financiers a return on their investment. You must pay interest – and repay capital – to lenders such as the bank. If there is spare cash, you and other shareholders may want to draw back any personal loans made to the business.

The cash flow generation of your business largely depends on how well you run your business. It is necessary to forecast your cash flow. The more warning you have of cash flow peaks and troughs, the more time you have to deal with them.

Accounting software makes it easier to prepare budgets and revenue and expenditure forecasts for the months and years ahead (see the section 'Setting up an accounting system' in Chapter 3). Prepare budgets showing the level of sales and profits you expect to achieve, and the costs involved in doing so. Estimate the sales and margins, based on past experience. Overheads such as rent can be accurately predicted.

BEING REALISTIC

Prepare monthly (or weekly) cash flow forecasts for the next year, and update these monthly. These forecasts show what cash you expect to come in, and when (if at all) you expect to run into problems. Identify the major outgoings, especially those on fixed dates, such as the monthly payroll. Make sure you will have sufficient cash on the day to cover each payment. Be realistic. For your regular sales, use the established figures for sales volumes, debtor periods and bad debts. For any new products or customers, be pessimistic – expect problems and delays, and do not book a sale until the customer has paid the invoice. Be aware that monthly forecasts do not take into account weekly fluctuations.

Monitor your actual performance against the budget and the cash flow forecast regularly. If you know you will be short of cash in three months' time, you might reduce stocks, slow down sales growth, or agree extended credit from a major supplier for that period. The only way to generate cash over the long term is through retained profits. By comparing your performance with the budget, you can quickly judge whether sales and profits are going to plan.

Essentially, today's sales are tomorrow's cash flow. If you need to improve your cash flow temporarily, adjust your sales and marketing plans to suit. Bring forward sales by offering customers discount incentives to purchase quickly. Good stock control can release substantial sums of money. Aim to maintain just enough of each type of stock to service your customers on an ongoing basis. Identify seasonal peaks and troughs. Set a target stock-turn (for example, six times a year) for each category of stock, then monitor your performance.

Security and pilferage

Crime has financial consequences for businesses and affects the quality of life of both customers and staff. You may not be aware of some initiatives that may help you. With this in mind the Department for Business, Innovation and Skills (BIS) has published two complementary guides on how to tackle crime against business. These are 'Crime Against Business – What Businesses Need to Know' and 'Crime Against Business – What Partnerships Need to Know'. 'What Businesses Need to Know' gives practical tips, including how you can get heard locally and how to identify the organisations that can help you tackle crime.

The recently formed Local Crime and Disorder Reduction Partnerships (CDRPs) and Community Safety Partnerships (CSPs) monitor crime levels and determine priorities in local areas. They ensure that police, police authorities, local authorities, fire authorities, primary care trusts in England and local health boards in Wales come together to establish the levels of, and address, crime and disorder.

Much crime against business goes unreported to the police for a variety of reasons but the Federation of Small Businesses (FSB) encourages businesses to report all crime to the police. When you report a crime, ensure you get a crime number so that you, or the local business crime reduction partnerships, can track the progress of the case. You can find out how to report a crime at www.direct.gov.uk/policingpledge. Your local police force can tell you if there is a business crime reduction partnership in your area. These partnerships will provide support, intelligence, crime reduction advice and practical help (such as CCTV) in order to assist your business in preventing or dealing with crime.

In addition, every area in England and Wales has a dedicated neighbourhood Policing Team consisting of police officers, police community support officers, special constables, local authority wardens, volunteers and other partners. Check details for your area at www.direct.gov.uk/neighbourhoodpolicing

SHOPLIFTING

Shoplifting has also become a large part of retail shrinkage, no matter how big or small the retail shop may be. You will need to identify shoplifters and shoplifting methods and create a less attractive environment for them. Become familiar with the categories of shoplifters, common shoplifting methods, and know what to look for in customers who exhibit strange behaviour. Shoplifters are either professional or amateur and can be quite skilled in the art of thievery.

Many work in groups of two or more to distract the sales staff while they pilfer. They take advantage of busy shops during peak hours or they may hit at times when employees are less alert, such as opening, closing and shift changes. Merchandise is concealed in the clothing of the shoplifter, in handbags, strollers, umbrellas or inside purchased items. Other methods include price label switching, short changing the cashier, phoney returns and so on.

There are some signs that can signal a shoplifter: customers who spend more time watching the cashier or sales clerk than actually shopping; those who wear bulky, heavy clothing or coats during warm weather; some take several items into dressing room and only leave with one; and someone who frequently enters the store but never makes a purchase.

Good store management is an effective preventative tool and you should use store layout and design to prevent theft. Design your shop so that customers must pass the payment area and staff to exit the store. Never leave your cash register unlocked or unattended. Do not display merchandise near the store exits. Use mirrors to eliminate blind spots in corners that might hide shoplifters. Have adequate lighting in all areas of the shop and put up signs and posters reinforcing security messages.

Customer service

Customer service is a number one goal in any long-term business relationship. Pay attention to your customers and sell what they really want. Treat your customers with respect and dignity at all times. Hands-on dealing with your customers is a crucial factor. An advantage of being a small business is that it is usually easier to respond quickly and personally to customer enquiries. If you put effort into keeping your customers content, they will remain loyal to your business.

Word of mouth recommendations made by satisfied customers are a powerful form of promotion and you should aim to provide a level of service that will help to bring this about. Happy customers not only tell friends and colleagues about you, they will also be able to tell you what your competitors are doing. Offer these customers a reward for recommending your business to others. Customer loyalty schemes, such as a voucher with a discount off the next purchase or 'buy three for the price of two', is an effective way of encouraging your existing customers to keep buying your products. Give key customers advance notice about offers coming up, or when you are planning something new. You should have as your motto: 'Once a customer, Always a customer.'

Ensure that popular products are always in stock and all enquiries are dealt with straight away. Keep your customers informed and ask them for feedback and listen to what they say. If there is going to be a problem, let your customer know straight away. If a customer complains, treat it seriously and deal with it efficiently and learn from them. There may be areas of your business you need to improve. Leave your customer satisfied with the outcome. If you are polite and handle the complaint well, you may even convert the complainant into a regular customer.

Personal service is always appreciated: addressing your customers by name when they come in and treating them as individuals can make all the difference. Exceed your customers' expectations and continually think of ways to build and improve goodwill between yourself and your customers.

Says Tom Algie of Practically Everything in Settle:

> *I listen to my customers all the time. I now have 20,000 lines, 15,000 of which I did not have when I first opened. The shop is called Practically Everything, which was the new name I gave to the Toolbox after I bought it, but the customer base was established then. Suppliers and salesmen who call also put you on to new things, but my suggestion would be don't buy too much of anything. Do listen to your customers. Do talk to other shopkeepers and others in the same trade in other towns. Read about your market and find good suppliers early.*

HAPPY CUSTOMERS

Delivering a high level of customer service also depends on holding on to good staff. According to the online forum Talking Retail (www.talkingretail.com), if you show care for your employees, they in turn will care for your customers. One way of improving staff retention, customer service, store standards and business efficiency is through staff training.

Staff in the front line of your business should be trained in the right personal and communication skills. Customer care relies on the spoken skills of your sales staff – without this your store can never be truly customer-friendly. Your staff should greet customers warmly, smile, make eye contact, and look and sound cheerful. They should be polite, friendly and speak clearly, show a personal interest and be helpful.

When offering product advice, think about the customer's needs. Make sure your appearance and that of the shop creates the right impression. Use reliable suppliers to make sure you have adequate stock levels. If you are out of stock of a particular product, offer to order it for the customer and keep your promise of delivery date. If there is a delay, inform the customer as soon as possible.

It may be a good idea to reward your staff for excellent customer service; they will feel valued and keen to make that extra effort. According to the *Harvard Business Review*, it costs up to seven times as much to find a new customer than to get more business from an existing one.

9
SPREADING THE WORD

The purpose of your business is to bring in customers and this can only be accomplished by marketing effectively. This is one of the most important factors in ensuring your shop's success and longevity. It is all about getting your message across. Guided by your own market research, analyse how you are going to reach your target market to convey your key sales message. People can't buy from you if they don't know you exist. You must have a clear picture of your business and the benefit customers will gain from buying your products. Pricing will also be essential to your marketing programme and your location is just as important.

This makes up the marketing mix and once you have a firm decision on your product, price and place, it will lead you to the construction of your marketing and promotion plans. As mentioned in the section 'Researching your market' in Chapter 2, a thorough evaluation of your competition and the anticipated strengths and weaknesses of your business will help to define your market.

Marketing is a term that basically means getting your business out to potential customers any way you can. There are many ways to do this, but among the more effective methods are:

☐ advertising;
☐ public relations;
☐ promotions;
☐ sending out press releases to obtain free publicity;
☐ mailing postcards or flyers;
☐ hosting a seminar or event;
☐ cross-promoting with another company that targets a similar audience;
☐ networking at industry or local business events;
☐ creating a brochure or newsletter;
☐ collecting names and email addresses for your database;
☐ launching an email marketing campaign;
☐ creating a plan that includes strategies that work for your business;
☐ developing a website.

Marketing plan
Firstly, draw up a marketing plan detailing the four Ps of marketing: your products and services, the place in which you sell them and the way you distribute them, the price you

charge, and the promotion you undertake. Another simple but effective method of planning your future is with a SWOT (strengths, weaknesses, opportunities and threats) analysis.

You can draw up your marketing plan by following these steps.

- ☐ Define objectives – what you need to achieve in financial terms and what you need to sell in order to get there.
- ☐ Take stock of resources by analysing the strengths and weaknesses of your business. List what equipment exists and what is needed.
- ☐ Create an identity and image – a name, style and logo.
- ☐ Plan how to project your image.
- ☐ Profile your products by understanding the benefits of your products and what makes people buy them.
- ☐ Project your buying patterns.
- ☐ Analyse your market place – how are your competitors doing, what is the state of the market and how far will your customers travel.
- ☐ Be aware of the importance of timing – launch new products at the right time.
- ☐ Determine a pricing policy dependent on market research, the competition, image and value for money.
- ☐ Design a promotional campaign.

 Your marketing budget should be largest in bad economic times, not in good times.

Grabbing attention through advertising

Building awareness of your shop is inextricably tied to your unique selling proposition (USP) – this is what makes you better than anyone else. Your USP could be a better service, more convenience, car parking, fast delivery, delivery to the door or a wider range of products. Be careful about simply competing on price. Your USP should focus on benefits, not features. Based on WIIFM (What's in it for me?), tell customers how your products will benefit them, not what they have to offer.

The three main aims of media promotion are to inform, remind and persuade your customers about your products, services and the shop itself. Make sure your target customers are reached by the media in which you advertise or promote yourself. How you tell people about your business will be determined by the type of customer and your advertising budget.

You can keep yourself in the public eye by advertising your shop in the local newspaper. Advertising is the art of telling people all about a business and what it can do for them. Your message must have an impact to cut a swathe through a myriad of other advertisements and special offers. The advertising department at your local newspaper will be able to give you advice on cost, the area they cover and their circulation. Make sure you understand the demographics of any media before you decide to advertise. This includes circulation figures, sample adverts, specifications for placing adverts, pricing and special offers.

ATTRACTING CUSTOMERS

The aim of your advertisement is to increase sales and attract additional customers, to introduce a new range of products and to tell people who you are and how you plan to assist them.

Concentrate on local magazines and newspapers first; getting national exposure can be difficult. Advertising in special features, such as one that puts the spotlight on local retailers, or highlights a specific area, can be useful. It is estimated that only 30% of local newspaper readers look beyond the headline of an advert, so what you say must grab their attention and create interest. This will then lead to a desire to visit your shop.

Readership of regional or local newspapers at 85% is higher than the readership of national newspapers at 67.7%. Free newspapers and community magazines have the geographical focus needed for shops. They are, generally, cheaper per advertisement and useful for test-marketing.

Trade and technical, and club and society magazines may also be suitable. Specialist interest magazines are particularly useful for promoting your shop and will appeal to your target market.

Advertising or listing your shop in the *Yellow Pages* (www.yelldirect.com) and *Thomson Local* (www.thomsonlocal.com) may also be advantageous. These and other trade directories have high circulations and long shelf-lives. Managing a general advertising budget properly means finding media publications that will maximise exposure at a reasonable cost. Getting radio or TV coverage is fantastic, but difficult unless you've got something remarkable to say or publicise. Features and mentions in magazine articles can give the most rewarding publicity.

PAY PER CLICK AND PIP

Pay per click advertising has developed into an ideal solution for business owners who have modest financial resources. Setting up internet advertising space means you can mix it with the big brands, tapping into huge advertising budgets.

Once you have registered with a search portal, you are invited to enter keywords and phrases. To make the most of this form of advertising campaign, start with a small number of keywords and dedicate the majority of the budget towards phrases garnering the most clicks. Choose a concise set of keywords, which accurately reflects the nature of your business and which targets customers who are genuinely interested in what you have to offer. Go through your website and pick out the most relevant terms. After deciding on key terms, the next step is to incorporate those keywords into the advertisement's text.

When the pay per click campaign is up and running, the next step is to employ more advanced functions such as time scheduling and advert targeting. Dedicating £3 per day to search engine marketing will open up a whole new world of sales opportunities.

Alternatively, a traditional tried and tested form of advertising is a package insert programme (PIP). These are advertisements inserted into packages being sent out by other retailers. In other words, if a shopkeeper sends lots of packages to customers, they sell space in these packages to other shop owners who want to advertise to the same customers. The going rate for these PIPs starts from £30 up to more than £50 for 1,000 packages sent. However, while this may be relatively cheap, response rates are lower than direct mail.

In-store advertising

Once you have developed your marketing and advertising strategy to draw people to your shop you should then advertise and promote heavily inside your shop. Many retailers now realise how important in-store advertising can be to their bottom line. This is based on the theory that customers go into a shop with one or a few key items in mind; the aim then is to entice these shoppers to buy more with well-planned advertising and marketing within the store.

In-store advertising can introduce new products by attracting attention through their look, feel or smell; promote sale items and impulse buys; and provide more information on featured merchandise. You should base your in-store advertising on positioning your products in an interesting way to catch the eye of your customers as they pass your displays. Make sure the advertisement areas are well lit. Thematic in-store advertising can focus around a specific season (for example, Mother's Day or Easter), a holiday, or even a new trend or fashion.

 Your advertising and the type of displays need to match the tone and ambience of your retail establishment.

Direct mail

Producing a professionally designed leaflet or brochure showing samples of your products is another way to reach your target market. Even if the costs of design, print and mailing can be high, it can be a useful tool for your business. A direct mail campaign can spread your message to potential customers, but the backbone of an effective campaign is the mailing list. This is where knowing your target audience is crucial. The more precise your list, the more effective your direct mail programme will be.

Compile your mailing list through your existing customers, the web, directories in your library, your trade association or the electoral role. Suppliers may also be able to suggest other prospects. Renting a mailing list may also be cost-effective: £100 to £120 per 1,000 names is normal. You can get a list of database members from the Direct Marketing Association (www.dma.org.uk) or in the *Yellow Pages* under 'direct mail'. You can also get more information from Royal Mail (www.royalmail.co.uk).

The only disadvantage, however, is that low response rates are a fact of life – 1% to 2% can be considered a success and many businesses do a lot worse than that. A handwritten address to a named individual with a stamp is the most likely way to be opened and read. Allow enough time for design, printing and mailing your piece. Design and printing can take anywhere from a few days to several weeks, depending on its complexity.

Press releases

As part of your marketing campaign, it is worth taking the time to prepare a press release to send to local or national newspapers, magazines or television. You can find a list of all the national and regional papers, magazines and broadcast media at www.mediauk.com

The press release must grab the reader's attention immediately and ensure that they will read on. Start with a snappy title and list all the key points that make your business special. Then decide on your message or unique selling point and consistently put that across. Start with the most salient points and use simple, direct language. A quote or testimonial from a customer or supplier is always useful. Including a photo increases your chances of coverage.

Think about what the media are looking for; they generally want a story, preferably one they haven't heard before. Find the journalist's name and send your correspondence to them directly. Convince them of why they should feature you. Your press releases should answer the journalist's five basic questions of Who? What? When? Where? Why? Follow the 'style' of the publication and add your contact details. You can always contact the same journalist again with reminders of seasonal products and special days, but don't overdo this as it can work against you.

Word of mouth

At the end of the day, the most cost-effective promotion is word of mouth. If satisfied customers recommend your business to friends, family and colleagues, it is advertising that money can't buy. Aim for this by consistently exceeding your customers' expectations, satisfying your customers with work well done, having a good relationship with your customers, building up a good reputation and protecting it by sorting out any problems quickly.

When SmallBusiness.co.uk posed the question: 'Which marketing strategy works best for your business' to their readers, they received the following response.

- Radio ads (0%).
- Sending email alerts (2%).
- Local newspaper ads (2%).
- Cold calling (7%).
- Sending direct mail (12%).
- Advertising online (15%).
- Word of mouth (62%).

Says Tom Algie of Practically Everything in Settle:

> ❛ *Take a low risk approach to opening your shop for six months between Easter and October. By then you should know if you stand a chance. Love your customers – they will come back and tell their families and friends. Use any opportunity for free publicity or to create some interest.* ❜

Data protection

The Information Commissioner's Office (ICO) is the UK's independent public body set up to protect personal information and promote public access to official information, from data protection and electronic communications to freedom of information and environmental regulations. You are legally obliged to protect any personal information you hold. If you are unsure about your responsibilities when launching a marketing campaign, the ICO guides will tell you everything you need to know.

If you hold and process information about your clients, employees or suppliers, you will need to comply with the Data Protection Act. This states that personal information must be kept secure, up-to-date and processed lawfully and fairly. You will increase customer confidence by ensuring that the information is accurate and thereby enhance your business's reputation.

If you process personal information you must notify the ICO, unless you are exempt. It costs £35 a year and failure to notify is a criminal offence. By notifying the ICO you join the Public Register of Data Controllers. In addition, you may also have a number of obligations under the Freedom of Information Act. If you are planning a marketing campaign using the telephone, email and other electronic marketing methods, the Privacy and Electronics Communications regulations apply and, once again, you need to make sure you comply with the regulations. For more information, see www.ico.gov.uk.

Developing a website

The internet is now a major force for businesses and is widely embraced as an excellent communications tool. The promotion of your website should be an integral part of your marketing strategy and your overall business plan. It is a vital tool for promoting your company and selling your products and services. It can also provide information for other people: suppliers, lenders and staff.

There are three kinds of website.

- ☐ Simple homepage – this works as a basic communication tool.
- ☐ Showcase website – if you want to expose a more detailed explanation of your product range.
- ☐ Online webstore – for online sales.

A simple homepage is a starting point to keep in touch with customers and to attract new ones who are browsing the internet. It should include your name and logo, a description of your business activity, summary of your products and service, photographs of your products, contact details, opening hours and a request for feedback. It is suitable for aiming at local customers and is a cost-effective option because it needs minimal maintenance.

A showcase website is the equivalent of putting your brochure online. It will contain the same information as a homepage but will include more pictures of your product range or product groups spread over a number of pages. You should keep it simple – don't make it difficult to load or the navigation too complicated. Update it regularly with new information and products. If you pay an outside company to host your website, make sure you can update as and when you like.

DOING BUSINESS ONLINE

An online webstore should be developed when you are ready to do business online. You will need to fulfil customers' orders from anywhere in the country within three days; deal with problems, late deliveries, refunds and exchanges; and operate secure debit and credit card payments. An effective e-commerce site should have the following elements:

☐ A clean, easy-to-navigate look that is consistent from page to page.
☐ Clear photos and descriptions of what you are selling.
☐ An easy-to-use checkout system, with credit card options.
☐ Information about your company and its policies (including returns and privacy).
☐ A method of contact – by email and/or telephone – for questions or customer service issues.

It is estimated that online spending by families with internet access at home is running at about £18 billion a year. Although overall online spending is up, growth has been confined to the clothing, footwear and accessories sector. UK shoppers are flocking to buy clothes online, especially lingerie. Figures from IMRG Capgemini e-Retail Sales Index (April 2009) reveal an 85% jump in clothing sales. The study also reports a 72% year-on-year growth in online lingerie sales.

Says Julia Reynolds, Chief Executive of Figleaves.com: 'Our experience tells us that retailers with strong brand values and a clear target customer will stand out during an unsure economic environment. To introduce changes in fashion seasons online, e-tailers need to communicate with customers and use various marketing methods. Email alone is no longer sucient.'

DESIGNING YOUR WEBSITE

Examine your business and decide what type of website you need. Consider whether you want to build and update the site yourself with an easy to set up and administer template-based service, or whether you need the help of a design agency. Your choice should be based on a combination of the level of sophistication you need in programming, the time you have available to build a site, and your budget.

If you feel confident enough to build the page yourself, there are many programs available, such as Microsoft Expression, Dreamweaver and Coffee Cup. Most packages offer templates or automated wizards to help you get started. Some providers offer off-the-shelf packages for £200 or so, followed by monthly fees of £20 or more to rent space for your site.

If you commission a web designer, you will need to create a detailed brief to help the designer to create a website that meets your needs. You will need the facility to make ongoing changes to your website, such as updating prices. Your designer may do this for you for a fee, but it may be cheaper to buy your own copy of the software to edit the content.

Your website should be quick to download, easy to navigate, up to date, and logical in organisation and structure. By law it must comply with the Disability Discrimination Act, which requires you to ensure it can be accessed by anyone with a disability. For more information, contact the Disability Rights Commission (www.drc-gb.org). You may also be affected by the Data Protection Act, if you collect, store or process personal data, and the EU Distance Selling Directive.

DOMAIN NAMES

The first step in setting up a website is to determine a domain name, or URL. This is the website address that people will type in to their web browser to get to your site. It is a unique address through which every website on the internet can be recognised. Domain names are generated from a huge variety of sources but a simple search engine search for 'domain name registration' will yield companies that handle website registrations. All domain names end up on a central register so that customers everywhere can find your website with the help of a search engine.

It is often beneficial to use your business name for your domain name (URL). If you do not choose this route, ensure you use a name that best represents your shop's interests. Some characteristics of successful domain names are that they are brief, memorable and distinctive. They can only contain letters, numbers and dashes. Do not include any hyphens and avoid confusion with another business with a similar name. Many of the more obvious names have been taken so it's worth coming up with a short list of acceptable names.

You can register your domain name through any number of domain name registration websites in the UK and it costs from about £3 per name a year. Your 'domain name registration' search will find those that provide name registration cheaply and others who include name registration as part of a package, including web hosting and email. If you register more than one domain name they will all point to the same site.

Choose a reputable domain name supplier. Several websites act as brokers. You can visit one of these sites and browse the domain names that are for sale or put in a request for the name you want if it ever comes up for sale. Brokers include www.Pool.com, www.Sedo.co.uk, www.Snapnames.com and www.Dotpound.com. Do not divulge a required name to anyone before registering as these can be monitored. You can check a name through www.myrequiredname.com. When you are ready to register your name, go to www.netbenefit.uk. The organisation that maintains the registry of domain names in the UK is Nominet (www.nic.uk). You can check the names that are unavailable and it has a good frequently asked questions (FAQ) section on all aspects of the naming process.

If you buy a domain name, make sure you also buy the other top level domains (TLDs) for the same prefix (for example, .com or .net). This will make sure that no one else can capitalise on your brand name at a later stage. You can buy a domain name through an online seller, such as 1&1 (www.1and1.co.uk) or UK2Net (www.uk2net.net). Domain names that are bought must be renewed every two years.

Remember, you don't own a domain name – you only rent it. A lot of small firms get their fingers burnt because they forget to renew their domain name. There is a whole industry out there engaged in 'sniping'. They sit and see that your domain name is going to expire and the second it does they have an automated piece of software to swoop in and buy it. Once they do this, you have no further right to it.

WEB HOSTING

A web-hosting provider will host your site on their space on the world wide web and make it available to the public. How your website is designed determines which web host to use. For example, if you have an Expression (previously FrontPage) website, you will need a web host which supports Expression. To find the right web host, check out the many web-hosting directories on the web. These directories are set up to allow you to search using the features that you are looking for in a web host. Decide on a few and then visit the many web-hosting message boards and forums. See if your potential host is listed and what other people's experiences have been with the host you have in mind.

Most web hosts have multiple plans you can choose from. Contact them and make sure that they provide the features you need. The majority require you to sign up by using a credit or debit card. Your internet service provider will probably also offer web hosting, but others include:

☐ www.spanglefish.com offer free websites (and hosting) with small Google ads on them. If you pay £25 per annum you can get rid of the Google ads and end up with an impressive site;
☐ Freezone Internet (www.freezone.co.uk) offers web hosting, design and domain names;
☐ www.1-2-3-reg.co.uk offers hosting from £1.48 a month.

GETTING NOTICED

To make sure your website succeeds, you must find ways to attract to your site customers who buy. To do this, consider including your web address on all of your shop's promotional materials, sending email blasts and postcards to prospective customers, buying sponsored links or adverts on Google or Yahoo!, posting useful blogs, and purchasing banner ads on well-trafficked sites. You need to generate publicity about your website both online and offline. Your website needs to be continually updated to keep it fresh, interesting and competitive.

Research shows that when people are searching the web, hardly anyone bothers to look beyond the first page of results even though the search often produces hundreds of them. So to get your company noticed, you need to give your website name enough pointers for it to be automatically placed on the first page of search results.

Once you register your site address, the search engine will scan and index your pages every few weeks or so. Software called a spider is used to crawl over your site looking for keywords known as metatags or meta descriptions. These keywords are then used to create your website's listing.

Use a search engine, such as Google, Alta Vista, Yahoo!, Lycos, Ask.com, or do your own keyword research through www.wordtracker.com. Google has a PageRank system where all web pages indexed by them are ranked. By getting your business in relevant business directories and being mentioned in online articles, you will increase your link popularity and improve your rankings. Adding new content and refreshing your site regularly will have the same effect. Search engines tend to reward sites with good quality content.

Search engines generally provide a free service (both indexing and retrieval) but it is time consuming. It may be worth spending between £50 and £100 with a specialist agency that will register your website as effectively as possible with all the best search engines and web directories. Type 'registering my website' into a search engine to find more details. You can also use a web directory such as iNeed, Yahoo! or ShopSmart, which use editors to review your site and create listings from descriptions you submit to them.

Says John Courtney of Strategy Consulting:

> *Some companies can charge anything from £1,000 to design and build your website but search engine optimisation is more important than the design and build, without it customers won't find you. You should spend more on the optimisation than the design and build.*

Apart from search engine optimisation, traditional forms of marketing are still applicable to e-business. The target customers may not be internet users or have any reason to expect an online service from you. A newspaper advertisement or flyer can be very effective in these cases. You can use a service like Google Adwords or Yahoo! Sponsored Search where you pay for a short advert and a link to your site to appear on their search pages. You are charged on a cost per click basis, so that you only pay when someone clicks on your advertised link.

Incorporate your website on all of your printed material: advertising copy, letterheads, business cards, email signatures, invoices. Your local press may be interested in any seasonal products or offers. Use newsletters to advertise special promotions or seasonal products. Your own network of contacts and customers are the best search engine of all. Word of mouth is a great way to persuade internet shoppers to surf their way to your site.

INTERNET SERVICE PROVIDERS

There are many internet service providers (ISPs) in the market that cater for business customers. Before choosing, consider the following questions.

- ☐ How many email addresses do they have for you to use?
- ☐ Can they host your chosen name?
- ☐ Do they provide access to templates and building site tools?
- ☐ Do they offer shopping cart facilities?
- ☐ What are the fees?
- ☐ What does the contract involve?

Remember that you can switch providers if and when you feel it necessary.

Look for a high-speed internet service that offers low contention, which means fewer other businesses are using the same service at the same time as you. Select a supplier and package that offers unlimited usage limits, even if you may only occasionally need it, as it is vital for business use – you would not want to hit a download limit or be charged extra for receiving a vital file.

Evaluate your own level of technical expertise, as this will have considerable bearing on how much support you need from a supplier. Consider whether your shop depends on being connected to the internet for its day-to-day running. If so, it may be worth considering a supplier that offers round-the-clock support, which should be included in the package with no hidden extra costs.

There is a lack of clear information about internet connections. While details of broadband speeds are readily available, other factors are not always made clear by suppliers, such as the effects that contention ratios (the ratio of other people sharing your connection) and the distance a user is from the exchange can have on download and upload speeds.

Although you can access broadband services via satellite or wireless, most consumers receive their service via the existing telephone lines (DSL), or via cable (Virgin Media) where the provider will run a cable into your property from the main street cable (or your existing TV cable). Download rates will be similar to the DSL service. The most popular type of DSL in the UK is Asymmetrical DSL (ASDL).

There is a blizzard of options, but the top reported ISPs are:

- ☐ PlusNet;
- ☐ Sky Broadband;

☐ Pipex;

☐ Virgin Media;

☐ BT Broadband;

☐ Talk Talk;

☐ AOL UK;

☐ Tesco;

☐ Orange.

Your ISP should be able to offer reliable connection speeds, faster downloads, good customer service and a competitive price. Consider the level of service you will get after a 12 or 18-month contract, rather than being swayed by advertising and introductory pricing offers.

Taking your business online

Online retailing is continuing to boom in the UK in spite of pessimism about the economy, according to a survey conducted by retail analysts Verdict Research (April 2009). The growth rate, the fastest in the previous six years, was about 10 times that of the UK's retail market as a whole.

But physical shopping is far from doomed. 'There is still a need and place for physical locations – the key is to ensure that synergies with online retailing are exploited to drive footfall to the stores', says Verdict. 'While having an internet presence is vital, giving the consumer choice by establishing strong links between the in-store and online offers is now essential.'

Taking your business online takes more than simply designing a functioning webstore. It will need careful planning and logistical preparation. You must be able to respond to email enquiries promptly and deliver your goods on time. This will maximise the sales and loyalty opportunities the internet presents. Respond by using an automated email response to let your customers know that you have received their enquiry. An email contact/ordering system could increase prospects and customers. For seasonal produce and specialities, customers will often travel outside their usual area to buy.

 Your webstore is open 24 hours a day, seven days a week and it is available to anyone, anywhere in the world. A number of software suppliers have introduced complete e-business solutions packages that can generate your shop front and supply all the supporting services including hosting and payment services.

You can get to know your customers by requesting registrations which will provide useful information, such as email addresses, postal addresses, product preferences and so on. To overcome resistance to registration, use special offers, new product details, newsletters and competitions. Make clear your commitment to maintaining confidentiality and non-disclosure of email addresses to third parties.

Your ordering process will need to include packaging, delivery, insurance and tax. You must set up a virtual shopping cart resulting in a simple single payment. The most popular form of payment is by credit card, but the processing is quite high risk so establish a merchant account with your bank, or use PayPal or WorldPay. Your customer's bank, your merchant account bank, your payment services provider and the credit card network (Visa/Mastercard) are all parties involved in a credit card purchase and each charge a fee. Compare the charges and services from site builders, payment service providers, hosting businesses, banks and IT companies before you 'set up shop'.

Ensure your site is constantly evolving. Keep it fresh with regular updates, special offers, accurate information about your products and service, and clear pricing and delivery details. This way you will drive repeat traffic. Make sure there are quick and easy steps to the checkout and emphasise your security and payment policies as reassurance for customers.

YOUR WEBSITE CHECKLIST

☐ Set your objectives, for example, marketing to existing or potential customers, providing product and sales support, making direct sales or recruiting employees.

☐ Look at competitors' and other websites to generate ideas. Develop an outline of what you want your site to include.

☐ Assess your technical requirements. For example, how large will the site be and will it use any special technologies, including product ordering and secure payment.

☐ If you are setting up a trading site, obtain merchant status allowing you to accept credit card transactions. Assess legal and liability issues.

☐ Check all in-house and outsourced back-up resources: dispatch and delivery, customer support, stock control and replenishment.

☐ Confirm your internet service provider (ISP) will be suitable for hosting your site. Check costs and the process for publishing and maintaining web pages.

☐ Source any technical or web design consultancy you need. Ask for references and evidence of the successful completion of similar projects. Make sure that design or copyright is assigned to you.

☐ Establish design guidelines in keeping with company style. Aim for visual clarity and easy navigation, avoid complex graphics that are slow to download, and consider developing a site that allows users to access a text-only version.

☐ Consider accessibility issues for disabled users and ensure compliance with the Disability Discrimination Act.

☐ Register your desired domain name.

☐ Build the site, ensuring that pages include appropriate keywords, metatags and page descriptions to help search engines list them.

☐ Test the site, using different versions of various browsers to ensure that pages download quickly and page links work.

☐ Assess the site's appeal and ease of navigation. Ask employees and key customers for feedback and suggestions.

☐ Launch the site. Register it with search engines to make it easy to find and identify other sites you can link to and from.

☐ Promote the site. Email target customers, for example, and include your website's address in your letterhead, brochures and advertising.

☐ Monitor usage and how effective the site is at achieving its aims.

☐ Keep the site up to date. Add new, time-critical material, particularly on the home page, to keep visitors coming back.

Using forums and networking

Informal networking, such as membership of your local Chamber of Commerce, Business Link, professional bodies or trade associations, can be very useful when working for yourself. Developing contacts and drawing on the expertise of others is paramount. You can forge alliances and obtain the know-how you may need to keep a competitive edge. Have clear objectives in mind when developing relationships as this can help to ensure they are beneficial to your business. When you go to a more formal networking event, such as a conference or trade show, arm yourself with some interesting news about your business.

Another business network is Entrepreneurial Exchange (www.entrepreneurial-exchange.co.uk) based in Scotland where you will find like-minded people who have created their own businesses and are generally risk-takers. Full annual membership costs £395, plus VAT.

It helps to be socially skilled if you are to make the most of networking opportunities. Good networkers do not force a relationship and will go where the energy is. Homogenous or personal networks that are too small will seldom produce startling results. If your network is not diverse, you will not make new contacts.

SOCIAL NETWORKING

An effective way of running your company more efficiently and making your market presence felt is to use social networking websites. A recent survey suggests 6,000 small businesses each day are using Twitter as a social networking site. Twitter is a rapidly growing web service, in which people can post small SMS-size snippets of information about anything they like.

Blogging has become an inexpensive, online social media tool and it is a powerful means of growing a business. If you are competing against big companies, you have to use whatever means you can to get your message out there and to tell people why you are different. Using these tools effectively, however, requires a different approach to traditional sales and marketing methods. It is more conversational in nature and is often slower-paced than traditional marketing campaigns. To find the influential websites, where products like yours are being talked about, use Google Alerts, which will tell you where a particular work or phrase is referred to online, or Google Insights for Search, which offers instant statistics on which people are searching. Then join the conversation.

CREATING A BLOG

Blogs can be a great way to promote your business and can be used as a powerful business tool. However, you must create a blog that has interesting, timely content, is visually attractive, and invites responses from its target audience. To make your blog stand out from the competition, do the following.

- ☐ Create a prominent link.
- ☐ Make sure a link is featured prominently on your home page if you want to generate traffic to your blog.
- ☐ The name of your blog should be easy to read and the date of that entry visible.
- ☐ It should be visually appealing.
- ☐ You need to post between 50 and 150 entries before you start getting response based on readership and traffic from search engines.
- ☐ Update your blog every two weeks at least.
- ☐ The aim of your blog is to learn more about what your customers or partners are thinking and how you can better serve them.
- ☐ Respond quickly to any responses to a blog post.
- ☐ Abide by the rules on business promotion using online tools.

There are a number of companies that will host a blog for you. These include Blogger, Moveable Type, MSN Spaces and Word Press. Typically, specialist and niche market retailers can benefit from blogs.

Trade shows

Trade shows and fairs can provide a direct route to customers and are great for networking and getting up-to-date on the latest products. Make sure the event will be attended by your target customers and check with the organisers about previous attendance statistics. Decide in advance which booths you want to visit. If possible, set up advance appointments to meet some of the exhibitors.

Peak visiting hours are generally between 10am and 2pm. Gather materials in advance and have your own material, from business cards to brochures, prepared and ready to go before you visit. If you intend buying at a trade show, be patient: you'll find that most sellers are willing to negotiate, especially if the show isn't packed and it's near the end of the day.

EXHIBITIONS AND TRADE SHOWS

- ☐ Clothes Show London, ExCel London, tel: 020 8267 8300, www.clotheshowlive.com
- ☐ Clothes Show Live, NEC Birmingham, tel: 020 8267 8300, www.clotheshowlive.com
- ☐ Convenience Retailing Show, NEC, Birmingham, tel: 01293 867 613 www.cstore-show.com
- ☐ Craft & Gift Fair, The Royal Cornwall Showground, Cornwall, tel: 020 8788 4434, www.edencrafts.co.uk
- ☐ Harrogate Lingerie & Swimwear Exhibition, Harrogate Int Centre, tel: 020 7973 6401, www.lingerie-show.com
- ☐ Home & Gift – Gift Trade Fair, Harrogate Int Centre, tel: 020 7370 8043, www.homeandgift.co.uk
- ☐ The National Wedding Show, Earls Court, London, tel: 020 7772 8316, www.nationalweddingshow.co.uk
- ☐ Natural & Organic Products Europe, Olympia, London, tel: 01273 645 110, www.naturalproducts.co.uk
- ☐ The Stitch & Creative Crafts Show, Edinburgh Corn Exchange, tel: 01822 614 671, www.sccshows.co.uk

10

RETAILING AND THE LAW

The average small business owner spends seven hours a week on red tape, according to the Federation of Small Business (FSB). Necessary paperwork includes forms for VAT, PAYE, National Insurance, health and safety, pensions, employment law and business rates. Finding the right information and advice can take much of the pain out of complying with legislation. Advice from good accountants and lawyers is vital in negotiating these thickets of legislation.

There is not a single comprehensive government agency dealing with everything you need to know. While there are resources like Business Link to help you, there is still a huge amount of work you have to do. Successive surveys by FSB have found that small businesses are by far more dissatisfied with the complexity of regulations, rather than the volume and cost of compliance. The vast majority of new regulations originate from the EU or central government level, but local authorities need to interpret and enforce the majority of them. The FSB believes that local authorities need to be sensitive to the challenges small businesses face in order to achieve compliance within a complex and changing regulatory regime.

The government is expected to introduce a new streamlined approach to the regulation of small business. This may mean exempting small businesses from some regulation where possible. Other approaches will include simple guidance and easy-to-use forms. The target is to reduce burdens by at least 25% by 2010 and, if this target date is met, it could make a vast difference when tackling complicated regulations.

According to the Confederation of British Industry (CBI), this simplification of regulation will include:

- removing regulations from the statute book, leading to greater liberalisation of previously regulated regimes;

- bringing together different regulations into a more manageable form and restating the law more clearly;

- using 'horizontal' legislation to replace a variety of sector-specific 'vertical' regulations and resolve overlapping or inconsistent regulations;

- reducing administrative burdens by simplifying forms and increasing the intervals between information requests and shared data.

Key legislation
The legislation you need to comply with when supplying goods or services to consumers includes the following:

SALE OF GOODS ACT 1979, SALE AND SUPPLY OF GOODS ACT 1994, SUPPLY OF GOODS AND SERVICES ACT 1982

This deals with consumers' rights and traders' obligations. The goods part of the legislation applies to goods supplied as part of a service, on hire, or in part-exchange. The goods supplied must be of merchandise quality and fit for any particular purpose made known to the supplier. The consumer is entitled to claim back some or all of her/his money from the trader if any goods do not meet these requirements.

The services part means a person providing the service must give the service with reasonable skill and care, within a reasonable time and at a reasonable charge. The consumer will follow a particular line of action if there is a complaint.

CONSUMER PROTECTION FROM UNFAIR TRADING REGULATIONS 2008

These regulations replace many of the existing laws (including most of the Trade Descriptions Act) since 26 May 2008. The new regulations ban traders in all sectors engaging in unfair commercial (mainly marketing and selling) practices against consumers.

If you intend trading online, you must be aware of the Consumer Protection (Distance Selling) (Amendment) Regulations 2005, which apply to contracts for goods or services purchased by a consumer where the contract is made exclusively by means of distance communication, either through mail order or internet sales. They outline both parties' rights to cancel a contract.

DATA PROTECTION ACT 1998

If you store personal details about your clients on your computer, you may have to register with the Data Protection registrar, which means your business is placed on a public register of data users. You are required to keep the information secure, accurate and relevant to your needs and to reply to requests from individuals for any information you are holding on them.

If you hold information about people on a database or in certain paper record systems, you may need to notify the Information Commissioner's Office (ICO, www.ico.gov.uk). You should contact the ICO to see of this is necessary and to find out about the strict requirements that need to be met under data protection legislation.

BUSINESS PROTECTION FROM MISLEADING MARKETING REGULATIONS 2008

These regulations have replaced the Trade Descriptions Act 1968 in respect of protecting businesses. They prohibit business-to-business misleading advertising and impose further restrictions on how businesses compare their products to rival products from other companies.

Food laws

Any business involving the preparation or sale of food is subject to a range of legislation governing labelling, safety, hygiene and traceability. If you intend selling food, The Food Standards Agency is the central government department responsible for food safety and hygiene legislation. You will also need to speak to the Environmental Health Department (EHD) in the borough, district or unitary council in which your business is located.

Says Bill Drennan of Food Law Policy Branch, Food Standards Authority:

> *The Environmental Health Officers (EHOs) will be able to give advice on hygiene and safety especially relevant to your business and are in the best position to determine which parts of food law apply to shops.*

You need to register with the EHD at least 28 days before opening. Contact your local authority for information on how to register. If you use two or more premises, you will need to register all of them. There is no charge for registering.

Key legislation includes the following.

- ☐ The Food Hygiene Regulations 2006 (England, Scotland, Wales and Northern Ireland) covers food hygiene, registration of premises, cleanliness, provision of equipment and facilities, temperature control and so on. This includes Hazard Analysis Critical Control Point (HACCP) safety management, which involves documenting safe practices.

- ☐ The Food Safety Act 1990 includes legislation to ensure that all foodstuffs are safe to eat and the description of food is not misleading.

- ☐ Under the Food Safety 1990 (Amendment) Regulations 2004 and the General Food Regulations 2004, all food businesses must establish a system whereby products can be traced back to the supplier. This means recording the name and address of the supplier, the nature of the products and the delivery date.

- ☐ The Food Labelling Regulations 1996 outline labelling requirements for most foods before delivery to the consumer, and apply to the packing and promotion of foods for human consumption.

- ☐ The Food Labelling (Amendment) Regulations 2004 brought the UK into line with a European Union Directive to inform consumers about possible allergens contained in food.

- ☐ The Plastic Materials and Articles in Contact with Food Regulations 1998 implemented European Directives relating to plastic materials and articles intended to come into contact with food. The Materials and Articles in Contact with Food Regulations 2005 set out further technical requirements for food packaging.

- ☐ The Weights and Measures Act 1985 covers requirements regarding units and standards of measurement.

The Trading Standards Institute (www.tradingstandards.gov.uk) has advice on a range of topics from food labelling to selling fireworks. Their online summaries include 'Price marking of goods for retail sale', 'Self assessment – a guide for licensees' (Scotland only), 'Advice to Chinese herbal medicine shops' and 'Business names'.

In addition, tobacco banning orders were introduced in April 2009 and mean that any retailer or staff caught selling tobacco products or cigarette papers three times in a two-year period to young people under the age of 18, could face a ban of up to a year, in addition to the penalties that already exist (a fine of up to £2,500).

Health and safety

You are responsible for the health and safety of your employees, visitors and customers.

If you employ staff, you should be aware of the Health and Safety at Work Act 1974, which requires you to provide necessary information, training and supervision to ensure employees' health and safety. You must display a HSE Health and Safety notice if you have employees. If you have five employees or more, you must have a written health and safety policy. You must ensure your premises are clean and safe and that all staff are trained in health and safety procedures. More information is available at www.hse.gov.uk

You must also carry out a risk assessment of your workplace. Health is just as important as safety, so consider noise levels, the lifting and carrying of objects and smoking policies. You no longer have to hold a fire certificate but you must show you have carried out fire-risk assessments and have adequate controls in place. Further information can be obtained from your local fire safety officer. There are many pieces of legislation you should be aware of that relate to the products you sell.

For online information on workplace safety, visit www.safeworkers.co.uk. This site contains more than 150 articles covering a wide range of specialist workplace safety issues, including discrimination, employment law, employment relations, finance, health and wellbeing. You can also ask a question and receive a reply published on the site.

Health and safety regulations cover a range of activities, such as working with Visual Display Units (VDUs), first aid, personal protective equipment, working at height and dealing with hazardous substances. Your legal obligations will depend largely on the products you offer but you will be subject to the following legislation.

THE HEALTH AND SAFETY AT WORK ACT 1974

This Act requires employers and the self-employed to provide a safe working environment for themselves, their employees and any other persons who may be affected by their activities. Minor offences can result in a fine of £5,000, while more serious offences can incur a fine of £20,000 or even six months' imprisonment. Extremely serious breaches can result in unlimited fines or a two-year prison sentence.

THE MANAGEMENT OF HEALTH AND SAFETY AT WORK REGULATIONS 1999

This requires employers to safeguard the health, safety and welfare of employees and clients and take the appropriate action to minimise or eliminate any risk.

WORKPLACE (HEALTH, SAFETY AND WELFARE) REGULATIONS 1992

These cover all businesses and require employers to:

- ☐ maintain the workplace and all equipment in a safe condition;
- ☐ provide adequate heating, lighting and ventilation;
- ☐ provide suitable toilets and washing facilities;
- ☐ maintain safe floors, staircases and passages;
- ☐ maintain fixtures, floors and fittings in secure and good condition;
- ☐ provide resting, eating and drinking facilities for staff;
- ☐ maintain fire exits and fire-fighting equipment;
- ☐ provide facilities for storing and disposing of waste safely.

ELECTRICITY AT WORK REGULATIONS 1990

Every electrical appliance must be tested at least once a year by a qualified electrician and a written record must be kept.

REGULATORY REFORM (FIRE SAFETY) ORDER 2005

This has removed the requirement for a fire certificate and placed more emphasis on the requirement for business owners to carry out fire risk assessments. The main stipulation of the legislation is that the person who has control over business premises must take reasonable steps to reduce the risk from fire and to make sure that people can safely escape if there is a fire.

Business legislation

2009 brought a flurry of new legislation and regulation for small businesses. Some of the main legislation includes the following.

THE HEALTH AND SAFETY OFFENCES ACT 2008

This Act came into force on 16 January 2009. It increases penalties and provides courts with greater sentencing powers for those who flout health and safety legislation. The Act raises the maximum penalties that can be imposed for breaching health and safety regulations and broadens the range of offences for which individuals can be imprisoned.

EXTENSION TO HOLIDAY ENTITLEMENT

As from April 2009, statutory leave has increased from 4.8 weeks' paid annual leave to 5.6 weeks. Bank and public holidays can be included in a worker's minimum holiday entitlement; alternatively they can be offered in addition to the minimum entitlement.

CORPORATION TAX

The controversial plan to raise small business corporation tax to 22% in April 2009, up from 21% in 2008, has been postponed until 2010. This stalemate also affects businesses with profits of up to £300,000.

EXTENSION OF TRADING LOSS CARRY BACK

Usually a company can carry back a trading loss that occurs in an accounting period for 12 months and offset the loss using profits gained from any source. New rules mean that companies can carry back their trading losses for up to three years, in certain circumstances, and for accounting periods that end between 24 November 2008 and 23 November 2009. Unincorporated businesses can make a claim for trading losses for the tax year 2008–09.

EMPTY PROPERTY RATE RELIEF

Properties with a rateable value below £15,000 are exempt from paying business rates. However, the empty property levy has not been scrapped. This affects owners of vacant properties that have a rateable value of £15,000 or more.

Disability discrimination

If you intend to employ someone, it is important to recognise how to avoid and prevent discrimination. There is direct discrimination (where you openly treat someone less favourably than you may others) and indirect discrimination (where you might place an unnecessary condition or requirement on a particular job to prevent certain people from applying).

The four Acts that focus on discrimination are:

- ☐ the Sex Discrimination Act 1975;
- ☐ the Equal Pay Act 1970;
- ☐ the Race Relations Act 1976;
- ☐ the Disability Discrimination Act 1995 (applies to companies with 15 or more employees).

With 10 million people living in the UK with a disability covered by the Disability Discrimination Act 1995, it is essential you keep up-to-date with your obligations. The law firm Addleshaw Goddard recommends retailers take note of the following recent amendment to the Act:

This extends the definition of disability to include mental illness, HIV, cancer and multiple sclerosis from the point of diagnosis and could mean a customer being entitled to bring a claim under the Act without staff realising.

As an employer, it is unlawful for you to discriminate against a job applicant or an employee with one of these conditions and you must also make reasonable adjustments to your premises.

While the size of your shop and the resources available to you will determine reasonable adjustment, it is important to be aware that you may have to look at alterations such as widening doors, installing ramps and altering counter heights. See www.direct.gov.uk/en/ DisabledPeople/index.htm and www.equalityhumanrights.com

Further information is also available from:

□ Office of Public Sector Information – www.opsi.gov.uk
□ Scottish Executive – www.scotland.gov.uk
□ Welsh Assembly Government – www.wales.gov.uk
□ Northern Ireland Executive – www nothernireland.gov.uk

11
LOOKING TO THE FUTURE

Your business focus will change as you move beyond the start-up phase. Good financial management, pricing, planning, preparation, research, awareness of competitors, insurance, location, advertising and promotions, advice and good customer service are all key to running a successful business. But every now and then, it is a good idea to stand back and review your shop's performance and the factors affecting it.

Identifying opportunities for growth

To ensure your shop's sustainability, identifying opportunities for growth becomes a priority. Create a plan for sustained growth. You can measure growth by looking at key statistics, such as your turnover, market share, profits, sales and staff numbers. A combination of sales and profits is the balanced way of measuring growth. If you are happy with your current performance, it is still important to keep looking for ways to develop, otherwise you risk allowing your competitors the room to grow and take market share from you.

Once you are sure that your shop is running efficiently, is properly structured and resourced, it is time to devise a successful growth strategy. You can diversify by adding new or related products to your existing range, establishing new products for existing products and services, and finding new products for new markets. While you do this, it is very important that you do not neglect your existing customer base. Be clear about development costs and don't lose track of or dilute your core products.

Decide if you need to employ people in weak areas or outsource some functions, such as marketing, sales, bookkeeping, accounting and tax. You may even wish to add more locations or franchise your ideas. Maybe your path to success just lies in making your business better. Look at improving profitability by reducing shrinkage, increasing sales opportunities, listening to your customers, improving customer service, buying from suppliers with the best value, increasing marketing, providing training for any staff members, and lowering expenses.

Retail Week offers the following survival tips.

- □ Bridge the gap. It is easier to cut costs than grow turnover to reduce losses and more agreeable to customers than raising prices.

- □ Use working capital for appropriate costs; finance refurbishments with a long-term loan.

☐ Think survival of business first, growth of business second. Look at the performance of individual locations/stock, not just the whole business.

☐ Consider planning, not just reviewing six months back or forward, but longer-term strategy.

☐ Ensure expansion is right. Don't pay too much for a long lease in the wrong location or you won't sell enough and it can be costly to get out.

☐ Toughen your stance on pricing/discounting. You are your suppliers' customer and they need your business, so haggle on price.

☐ Manage honestly. Take off rose-tinted spectacles and pull heads out of the sand.

☐ Act now and get quality help. Problems don't go away, they only get worse if you ignore them.

Lack of finance and cash flow, unexpected bad health, not keeping promises, greediness, poor admin and business practices, over reliance on one supplier, a lack of customers, apathy and complacency all force failure.

Building a business from scratch and watching it thrive is very rewarding. By seeking the proper knowledge and support, and applying hard work and excellence to the products you provide, you are on your way to success in the exhilarating world of retailing. Go get 'em!

Closing shop

Deciding to sell or close your shop will be a taxing time. You could have reached this decision for a number of reasons. The process of winding up the business should be viewed as an opportunity to protect the initial investment and any subsequent profits and to enable you to move on. Like any aspect of running a business, the better you plan the process, the better the results you will achieve. It will take time, good organisation and patience. The objective is to close the shop professionally and thoroughly and at the least cost (or even to maximise profits).

The first thing to do is to consider selling the shop as a going concern. Contact an agent to find out what options are open to you to sell your business complete. A profitable going concern could find a suitable buyer. Your accountant, solicitor or property agent can advise you who to contact to market, sell and transfer the business. You will need to prepare accounts and profit and loss statements, a weekly and monthly sales analysis covering the last two years, a list of assets, and some information on the potential of the business.

You are selling the assets and the potential, so you will need to value your business according to the location and condition of your premises, the length and value of the remaining lease, previous profitability, and value of stock and equipment. Someone could be interested in taking over your lease, so do consider selling it – if your lease has that option. If it doesn't, you will have to discuss suspending your lease with your landlord. This will cost you – at the very least to pay your landlord and your legal costs.

You will need to sell your stock; try and get its purchase value. A sale is a good idea – start at 30% to 50% discounts and move up or down. It is easier to have generic mark-downs (30% off everything) rather than individual lines. Get an accurate stock valuation and make sure all your stock is clearly marked with a retail price. Sell your fixtures and equipment and tell your suppliers what your plans are so that your supply can be stopped or altered for new owners. As soon as staff and suppliers know of the changes, you should advise customers and start your sale and mark-downs.

Finalise all payments regarding VAT, income tax, pensions, National Insurance and equipment lease arrangements. Advise HMRC (www.hmrc.gov.uk), contact your utility providers and disable any security.

More information is available at the British Chambers of Commerce (www.britishchambers.org.uk), which has a section on selling and buying businesses. Alternatively, contact Business Link (www.businesslink.gov.uk).

12
TYPES OF SHOPS

There are many types of shops you might want to choose from for your own niche. After you have chosen your main category, you need to decide the type of accessories that will go well with your choice. Think of ideas for offering accessories, special services or repair services to bring customers in. Visiting trade shows and gift fairs will give you a wonderful amount of choice. If your choice of a niche category (or categories) is a good one, with no competition and lots of potential customers, then you know you have a winner. Here is a selection, but there are others.

☐ Antiques.
☐ Art.
☐ Bicycles (and accessories).
☐ Books (new or second-hand).
☐ Bridal (and accessories).
☐ Cards (and wrapping paper and ribbons).
☐ Carpets.
☐ Clothes (men's and women's apparel and accessories).
☐ Collectibles.
☐ Computers.
☐ Convenience.
☐ Cosmetic.
☐ Crafts.
☐ Delis.
☐ DIY.
☐ Electrical.
☐ Fairtrade.
☐ Fancy goods.
☐ Farm.
☐ Fashion accessories.
☐ Fishing tackle.
☐ Florist (accessories and planters, artificial and dried flowers).
☐ Fruit and veg.
☐ Furniture.
☐ General.
☐ Gifts.
☐ Health.

- ☐ Jewellery (fashion and fine).
- ☐ Lingerie.
- ☐ Mobile phones.
- ☐ Models.
- ☐ Needlecraft and knitting.
- ☐ Office products and stationery.
- ☐ Outdoor equipment (camping, hiking and accessories).
- ☐ Pets.
- ☐ Picture framing.
- ☐ Shoes (and accessories).
- ☐ Sports.
- ☐ Sweets.
- ☐ Toys (and children's apparel).

From this list I have selected eight sectors to expand on as broad examples. They are:

- ☐ bicycles;
- ☐ bridal;
- ☐ clothes (women's);
- ☐ florist;
- ☐ health;
- ☐ jewellery;
- ☐ office products and stationery;
- ☐ toys;
- ☐ fairtrade.

Opening a bike shop

The Outdoor Industries Association (OIA) recently published research looking at the changing habits of the UK's outdoor consumers. Walking remains the most popular outdoor activity (91% participate regularly), but huge numbers of consumers are also road cycling (29%) and mountain biking (22%) regularly. Next are mountaineering (15%), skiing/snowboarding (14%), off-road running (13%) and climbing (13%).

CYCLING IN THE UK

According to the Association of Cycle Traders (ACT), there are approximately 2,000 specialist cycle retailers in the UK and Ireland, excluding Halfords, supermarkets and other general retailers. These specialist retailers represent about 40% to 45% of market turnover of approximately £750–£900 million annually. It is estimated that nearly 2.5 to 3 million bikes are sold in the UK annually.

It is highly diverse sector encompassing retailers of all shapes and sizes split into a number of different categories, the most common being:

- ☐ family/leisure – low to middle-priced bikes for adults and children;

☐ specialist shops – mountain bike, road, touring or recumbent, primarily for enthusiasts and regular commuters/leisure riders;

☐ hire shops/centres – some retailing involved but mostly cycle hire and they are often part of or near holiday centres and national parks.

Says Mark Brown of ACT:

> ‘ *Cycling is currently a "hot topic" on the political and social agenda, and increasingly promoted as a healthy, fun and cost-effective way to improve well-being and support the environment for all age groups. Mountain bike (MTB) and road are also gaining increasing profile and investment. This helps to position cycle retailers as important locally-based specialists – destination retailers – able to help people make the most of bikes and cycling.*
>
> *The Government is increasingly investing in and supporting the development and promotion of cycling both nationally and locally through a variety of projects and initiatives, which include creating more cycle routes (Sustrans), creating a number of Cycling Demonstration Towns, as well as educating school children about cycling skills, providing tax incentives to employers to promote cycle usage, and investing in a national celebration of cycling – Bike Week – to prompt more people to cycle.*
>
> *Today's bicycles are seen by many people as another price-driven commodity sold by supermarkets, non-specialist retailers and mail order providers. This means that specialists are under more pressure than ever before and are working harder to demonstrate their unique value to customers. Many consumers believe a £79.95 bike is a bargain and taking it away in a box just adds to the convenience; the skills necessary to build and maintain a cycle are often neglected.*
>
> *Large corporate chains have the marketing muscle to get their brand name into the majority of consumer minds and the buying power to get the best prices with the resources to ensure it all runs smoothly. Combine these commercial pressures with the seasonal nature of the market – a wet summer isn't good for cycle sales – plus the ongoing demands of running a small retail business in an industry with typically low profit margins, and what seemed like a great idea in the pub doesn't feel quite so much fun now the reality has kicked in!'* ’

ACT believes that modern cycle retailers must integrate their passion with some good straightforward business sense and an innovative approach to developing a niche retail business. In today's competitive market specialist retailers cannot compete on price alone – but if you are clever you can make your strengths work to your advantage. Specialists have a lot to offer – good quality product, a commitment to great customer service and that personal touch which big corporate retailers just can't offer, plus local involvement and specialist skills. Effectively employing all of these can give you an edge over the competition and help you win and keep customers.

As in other retail sectors, the location of your new shop is absolutely critical and will determine who your main target market is and what products and services you need to offer, plus what, if any, competition you may encounter. When researching the site consider the following important questions.

- ☐ How accessible is the site, for customers and deliveries/ collections etc?
- ☐ Is there space for test rides of new bikes?
- ☐ Is there ample room for cycle and car parking?
- ☐ Is it near other shops, schools, railway or other leisure/high footfall areas?
- ☐ Where is the nearest other bike shop and what sort of shop is it?
- ☐ You must carefully analyse any other shops in the area – what products and services do they offer, what are prices like, what type of customers do they attract and how well established is the business. What do these other shops do well and where do they fall short?

Says Mark Brown:

❛ *Ideally you do not want to be competing head-to-head with any other shops and preferably working together to help your business in the long run. Remember that premium bike brands often operate "territories" which means if another local shop has the brand you want, you may not get supplied.* ❜

Five miles is considered to be about the average distance someone will travel to their 'local' bike shop – however enthusiasts will often be prepared to travel a lot further. Local council and tourism websites should have this information. What is the level of local support, provision and involvement or interest in cycling? For example, are you part of a Cycling Demonstration Town or is there a good network of cycle routes and paths or off-road riding facilities. Many towns and cities have strong cycling cultures and local councils are increasingly keen to promote cycling. Local cycle routes are also great opportunities for shops to capitalise on.

What are the different demographics of the area? Are people generally affluent or are incomes lower? This will help decide what products and services you offer and at what level you promote your shop. Are there any local restrictions on deliveries, access or opening hours?

THE SHOP

When you decide where to locate your shop, ensure you give a great deal of consideration to the premises and retail environment. Ideally you want your new premises to give you sufficient room for growth as your business develops. However, you don't want lots of empty space which you cannot stock with products and which is therefore an expensive added overhead. It is usually easier to grow than it is to shrink, but it can be a fine balancing act.

The classic bike shop with the 'wall of steel' image – every available bit of space crammed with bikes and bits – is traditionally a put-off for many customers and will eventually impact on your income, by reducing what products and services you can offer and deterring customers rather than enticing them through the doors. Presentation is everything, especially if you want to sell good brands at higher prices. Ideally give your store an identity that is unique and makes people want to come back.

ACT recommends you ask yourself the following questions.

☐ Is there plenty of space for new deliveries and storage? Ideally this area needs separate access from the main shop to avoid wasting space and disrupting the sales area.

☐ Is there sufficient room for a fully functioning workshop? Servicing and repairs should ideally be undertaken away from the main part of the shop to give ample space for work to be undertaken. Remember, repairs and services are highly profitable functions – more profitable than bikes – so don't undermine them.

☐ Is there room for bikes awaiting repair and collection? Bikes are not always collected on time so they need to be stored securely.

☐ If you stock clothing, make sure there is a changing room.

☐ Is there a private area for staff with suitable facilities?

☐ Is there space for an office? Ideally the shop needs a secure area for files and computers, as well as for any private meetings.

☐ Does your lease give you an opportunity for expansion?

☐ Ideally your shop needs flexible display systems which can accommodate the variety of products you may stock. Remember, you are selling cycle products not shop fittings. Set a realistic budget and select flexible and modular fittings, which you can gradually develop and upgrade as your business grows.

☐ Planning your product range and the space it needs, such as the average number of bikes on display, ensures that you are making maximum use of shop fittings and space and meeting the needs of your stocking plan. Suppliers may often provide free or on-loan fixtures when stocking particular lines, so make the most of these where appropriate but don't force them into the shop just because they are on offer.

☐ The workshop area should be given equal attention to the sales floor. Don't be misled into thinking an odd corner to prepare a bike for sale or repair will do.

THE WORKSHOP

Workshops can and should make a positive contribution to turnover, rather than being an under-priced service that becomes a drain on resources. Not only can the workshop and your technical services be highly profitable, they can also help you to establish a key USP and are a great way to win customers. In addition, when the sales are slow your workshop should help to keep things ticking over.

Setting up the workshop must be costed carefully as professional tools can be expensive, while layout needs to be carefully considered to ensure maximum use of space. Investing in good quality tools ensures workshop jobs are done properly and efficiently, reducing damage, wastage and time. Many shops will have used tools for sale, which are worth considering if they are in good condition.

Here is a summary of results from ACT's 2008 workshop survey, which are worth considering in relation to your new business.

The business of running workshops

- ☐ Workshop-generated income contributes on average 24% of total turnover.
- ☐ Over 70% of specialist cycle retailers state that workshop turnover is increasing.
- ☐ Lack of space is the biggest challenge to workshop development.

Pay and training

- ☐ The average wage for a mechanic is less than £14,000 a year.
- ☐ Over 60% of cycle shops currently employ mechanics with Cytech qualifications (see information below under 'Training').

Pricing and services

- ☐ Workshop labour charges are increasing.

- ☐ More than 50% of shops charge more than £20 per hour for labour.

- ☐ The three most common workshop jobs are fitting and/or replacing an inner tube, new bike build and pre-delivery inspection (PDI).

- ☐ Price competition is not a material factor in the development of workshop business.

- ☐ Retailers need to be more confident with regard to introducing clearer pricing, especially for higher priced jobs, in order to promote strongly their true differentiator of service and value.

- ☐ If the workshop is visible to customers it will almost certainly reflect on the professionalism of the business, so make sure it works for you and not against you.

- ☐ How to find the right suppliers is one of the most common questions ACT is asked. A dominant factor in cycle sales is brand name and therefore early assessment of key suppliers and access to their product lines is imperative. However, there are many new shops opening each month so be prepared to differentiate and prove yourself to prospective suppliers. Sharing part of your business plan and the strength of your financing with suppliers is a positive step towards gaining the early support of suppliers.

☐ You also need to consider that some leading brands operate territories to protect existing accounts and to avoid duplication and over-supply in any one area. This may result in your shop not being able to gain access to all the brands you want.

☐ This is where careful analysis of local and regional competition is relevant to ensure you know which brands are being stocked where. Understanding your target market is also important in ensuring you establish the right relationships with suppliers who provide the right product for your customers.

☐ Developing a close partnership with a handful of key suppliers is generally considered the best way forward, especially in the early days. Consider just two or three bike brands and just a handful of parts, accessories and clothing suppliers. Less is certainly more in this context, enabling you to gain their support and commitment for your business. This approach will also enable you to specialise in the brands you stock and thereby gain a good reputation locally for those brands. Ultimately, performance, purchase volumes and regular payments will prove the value of your account with any supplier.

TRAINING

People are at the heart of specialist retail and will be your greatest asset. Making the most of your people will be a crucial factor in the long-term success of your business.

Training is now an increasingly important area for cycle retailers. There are two main reasons for this. Firstly, better-trained staff can provide a better service, which equals increased turnover with greater efficiency and improved profitability. Investing in training helps develop staff to enable them to offer customers the right services, while also demonstrating to your staff that they are a valuable part of your business.

Secondly, promoting recognised qualifications and your investment in training is a great way of telling customers you care about high standards and good service. It will help give customers peace of mind and it is also a useful way of attracting new members to your team. Recognised qualifications and accreditations also help to differentiate your business from the competition, especially non-specialist cycle retailers. Qualifications also provide useful back-up for retailers in cases of fault and error where expertise is called into question.

At present the majority of training and qualifications focus upon technical skills, which is no surprise given the nature of the products and services specialist cycle shops offer. Retail training courses are coming online under the Cytech (www.thecyclingexperts.co.uk/cytech/) banner. Cytech is the industry-recognised training and accreditation scheme for cycle retailers and their staff, and is endorsed by ACT and leading cycle manufacturers and suppliers. Cytech is the only qualification which has been developed specifically for cycle retailers, offering a range of options all with varying levels of complexity to meet the needs of your business.

Cytech qualifications can be obtained with government funding – where candidates are under 25 years old – and also by self-funding. ACT members and ActSmart subscribers can save money on the costs of training courses. When considering undertaking any form of training it is important to explore your reasons for doing so and what benefits you wish it to bring to your business as well as the time and costs involved.

The above section on Opening a Bike Shop has been supplied courtesy of the Association of Cycle Traders (ACT) and can also be found on its website at www.thecyclingexperts.so.uk

JOINING ACT

ACT is a membership organisation providing independent bicycle dealers, hire centres, cycle workshops and their suppliers with essential services to help support, develop and promote their businesses. It is also active in developing new initiatives, such as Cytech, The Cycling Experts, Fetch, and Bike Hub, which provides the entire sector with new opportunities for commercial development and promotion, while also endeavouring to support the long-term future of cycling.

Opening a bridal shop

There are about 1,300 bridal retail shops in the UK, even though fewer people are getting married each year, and others are choosing overseas locations where the wearing of non-traditional outfits is popular. You will also have to compete against the trend of buying second-hand wedding dresses.

However, a good quality, specialised and professional service will attract customers from outside of your immediate area even if you are competing with the bridal departments of stores such as Debenhams. It is essential that you deliver on time to fulfil your orders – prospective brides, bridegrooms and parents spend a huge amount of time, emotion and money preparing for their wedding day so you can't let anyone down. Concentrate on offering an exemplary service.

Your shop should be located in an area where you will have lots of passing trade, high visibility and sufficient parking nearby. Maybe even near a beauty salon, hairdresser, florist, cake shop, photographer or clothes shop. It should be able to accommodate a few dressing rooms and have good display mirrors and flattering lighting. Remember, most wedding dresses are quite bulky and you will need several rows of racks to display them. Make sure you lease a store space with ample room so your bridal shop won't look crammed and crowded.

 Decide whether you are going to offer a couture service or a budget range of wedding dresses. Essentially, you will need to cater for the first time bride and for the mature bride getting married for the second or third time. No bridal salon is complete without a wide variety of dresses in lots of different styles and sizes.

SELLING GOWNS AND ACCESSORIES

Once you have an inventory of dresses and catalogues from various designers, it is also important that you also sell bridal accessories, such as jewellery, headpieces, hair accessories, veils, shoes, bags, gloves and even underwear so that your customers can plan their total look in one go. You should also cater for other members of the bridal party – groom, mother of the bride and bridesmaids. There are more than 50 bridal suppliers but you could start off by contacting the following:

- ☐ Amanda Wyatt, 14 Deanway Business Park, Wilmslow Road, Handforth, Cheshire SK9 3HW, tel: 01625 522 347, www.amandawyatt.com

- ☐ Halo & Co, 210 High Street, Prestatyn, Denbighshire LL19 9BP, tel: 01745 859 730, email: sales@haloandco.com, www.haloandco.com

- ☐ Mon Cheri UK, Unit 30 Norman Way Industrial Estate, Over, Cambridge CB4 5QE, tel: 01954 232 102, email: weddings@mon-cheri.co.uk, www.mon-cheri.co.uk

- ☐ Mori Lee (UK) Ltd, 8/9 Hollis Road, Grantham, Lincolnshire NG31 1QH, tel: 01476 541 116, www.morilee.com

- ☐ Sincerity Bridal, Clifton Court, 48 High Street, Newport Pagnell, Buckinghamshire MK16 8AQ, tel: 01908 615 511, www.sinceritybridal.com

The main wedding season takes place between April and September but planning and ordering takes place many months earlier. Once you have a confirmed order, ask for a deposit of between 25% and 50%. When the wedding dress arrives, arrange a fitting and discuss whether any alterations are required. You could charge extra for this or include it in the original price. You may even wish to work to an appointments system, whereby the bride can get your undivided attention and advice.

Weddings are expensive celebrations and you need to make sure you price your wedding dresses and accessories correctly. Mark-ups are generally as high as 100%. The following are rough estimates.

- ☐ Gowns: from £500 to £1,000.
- ☐ Designer gowns: from £1,000 to £4,000, or more.
- ☐ Veils: from £45.
- ☐ Shoes: from £45.
- ☐ Tiaras: from £45.

GETTING THE WORD OUT

Now it is time to start marketing your business. Advertise in bridal magazines, attend wedding conventions and exhibitions, and drop off marketing materials at popular wedding venues. Do whatever you have to do in order to get your business known. Joining your trade association will keep you up-to-date with developments. While it is not immediately helpful, you can join the Retail Bridalwear Association (RBA, www.rbaltd.org.uk) when you have been established for more than five years.

Says Philip Rathkey, Secretary of RBA:

> ❝ *The main aim of the RBA is to set standards in the bridal retail trade in order to enable the public to "shop with confidence" in an RBA store. The five-year term was set as a significant proportion of new businesses fail within that time, so to achieve five years is a mark of particular distinction and gives confidence for the future.* ❞

The Bridal Industry Suppliers Association (BIS, www.bisassociation.co.uk) represents manufacturers, wholesalers and importers of bridal goods.

Opening a clothes shop

If you are obsessed with fashion, this could be the time to open a clothing shop. According to a Mintel report from 2008, the UK clothing market has been dominated by price for much of the last ten years, as cheaper sourcing from the Far East has facilitated the growth of value retailers and increased competition in the marketplace. Consumers are ever more demanding of price, quality and styling.

In womenswear, classics are back as British women are becoming tired of fast fashion. Exclusive Mintel consumer research (2008) shows that one in more than three British women (31%) cannot justify the cost of keeping up with latest fashions. Today, there is a growing trend towards better quality clothes with greater longevity. Mintel estimates the market for all womenswear retailing to be worth £21.2 billion.

ANALYSING YOUR COMPETITORS

It is difficult for small clothes shops to be competitive with national chains and department stores. However, small shops are more focused on the community. You will know your customers better, give terrific service, and have a more interesting collection of clothes on your shop floor that will add to customers feeling special. Yet, you will still need to analyse whether there is demand for another clothes shop in your area by counting all the outlets, including sports, outdoor and leisure shops. Supermarkets, such as Asda and Tesco, also offer a range of clothing. If there is a gap in the market then capitalise on it. Whether you decide to specialise in exclusive designer labels, high-end fashion or sport casual merchandise, never lose sight of what sets you apart from the other apparel stores. Specialising, or finding your niche, is crucial to your success.

You can choose from a broad range of categories to stock, including swim and beach wear; hats, scarves and gloves; underwear, lingerie and hosiery; jackets and coats; trousers, skirts and dresses; shirts, t-shirts, jumpers, cardigans and blouses. There are also accessories, such as handbags and belts, sunglasses, costume jewellery and footwear.

As with the start of any other business, locate your shop where there is a lot of passing trade. The casual passer-by is more likely to grow curious about a clothing store that looks attractive, charming and inviting. Your shop's appearance should portray a bright and modern image and be fitted and decorated professionally. Keep your shop well stocked. Have large, clean windows that showcase your clothing, with regular changes. It your shop exterior lacks personality, the casual person walking past will not feel a compulsion to step inside. You want to get as many customers into your shop as you can and the easiest way to do this is to make the storefront attractive.

Christmas is generally one of the busiest times and, traditionally, the two sales periods are January and early summer. Fashion changes very quickly, so take advantage of sales when you can. These days, sales seem to be held all year round but don't have too many sales periods as customers will wait for these rather than buying items at full price.

Determine such aspects as store hours, pricing and return policies. Consider e-commerce or credit card acceptance, special orders and gift-wrapping. You will also have tremendous competition from online retail specialists and e-commerce websites, including eBay. Therefore, it is imperative that you visit fashion shows, business expos and trade events to keep in touch with the latest fashion and trends. Read fashion magazines and trade publications for up-to-date news and articles. For membership details on your trade association, contact the Association of Suppliers to the British Clothing Industry (ASBCI, www.asbci.co.uk).

Remember that Coco Chanel went from being a little hat shop in Paris to international superstardom.

Opening a florist shop

The cut flower industry is worth £2.2 billion and is set to keep growing. About £1.3 billion is spent by people buying flowers and plants for themselves rather than as gifts. Given this growth, and the lure of working with a wonderful, creative product, it isn't too surprising that people want to start their own flower business, says the Flowers & Plants Association.

While the UK public may well have spent £2.2 billion on flowers a year, they spend two-thirds of that money in a supermarket, not with a high street florist. The most popular reason for buying flowers is for the home or place of work rather than for any special occasion, and the supermarkets have taken much of the 'passing trade' from traditional florists. However, people will still go to a florist for special occasions, for events, and also because a small florist can offer more unusual flowers and more expertise. In addition, as the market grows, supermarkets are using the expertise and creativity of florists to develop their own ranges.

Says Sarah Holland, Communications Manager at the Flowers & Plants Association:

> *There is more than one way to be a florist. The most popular route into floristry is to open a retail shop, but florists can also work freelance from home or from a studio. Freelance florists often work exclusively on events or contract work such as weddings. There are advantages and disadvantages to both – freelancing can have more flexible hours and location, but it does not have the variety of work and visibility of a shop on the high street.*

Bear in mind that the type of business you choose should also reflect the demands of your local market – they are your customers and will ultimately dictate whether your business is a success. Research your own intended location very carefully as the industry is fragmented and what works in one town will not necessarily work in the next.

TRAINING

No matter what kind of florist you choose to be, training is a must. Training can either take place at college or through on-the-job training in a florist shop. College training can be full-time, part-time or evening classes depending on the time you have available. For a full list of colleges offering floristry training, visit www.lantra.gov.uk. There are also a number of private courses you can do: check www.flowers.org.uk for details on education and training.

Says Amanda Hartley of Amanda's Blue Orchid Florist in Hull:

> *After working in a florist shop as a Saturday girl from the age of 14, I decided to go onto college and take floristry apprenticeship. After my apprenticeship ended, I had several different florist jobs to achieve more experience. By the time I was 19, I found that the things other shops were creating were boring and not what I would have liked to have received myself. I was also bored of doing the same things over and over again, so I decided to open my own shop.*

Training 'on-the-job' is often a good way to learn and experience retail floristry. The government has launched a Modern Apprenticeships (MAs) scheme for floristry, training programmes that individuals (aged 16–24) can carry out while doing their chosen job – so they are in a real working environment from day one and get the chance to earn money while they are training. MAs are also government-funded, which means they are completely free for the candidate and their employer. There are two levels of apprenticeship in England: a Foundation Modern Apprenticeship, which includes a NVQ (National Vocational Qualification) at Level 2, and an Advanced Modern Apprenticeship, which includes a NVQ at Level 3. Contact Lantra for further details.

SUPPLIERS

Once trained, you will need to start putting together the building blocks of your business and, obviously, good suppliers are essential. There are effectively four methods of purchasing flowers wholesale in the UK:

Wholesale flower market

New Covent Garden Market in Vauxhall is the UK's only dedicated flower market. It operates six days a week and houses a large number of flower wholesalers – the choice of wholesaler is up to you. In other parts of the UK, there are usually flower wholesalers within the local wholesale fruit and vegetable market (see full listing on the Flowers & Plants Association's website), or ask at your local Chamber of Commerce for details.

Flower cash and carry

These wholesalers are individual cash and carry-type wholesalers, not necessarily based within a market. There are numerous wholesalers of this sort in cities all around the UK – check in your local *Yellow Pages* under 'florist supplies' for details.

Dutch van

Due to our proximity to Holland (the flower centre of Europe), there are a number of 'flying dutchmen' who also supply the UK's florists. These are large, cooled vans filled with fresh flowers (bought that morning in the Dutch auctions) which visit your location on a given day – you simply buy 'off the van'. Some market wholesalers will also offer a van service.

Direct ordering

There are a number of companies that are able to offer direct ordering into the UK. An order is placed with them and the stock is bought on your behalf from the Dutch auctions. It is then delivered on a set date and time to your location. The system usually works via a password-controlled website.

DETERMINING YOUR SPECIALISATION

Before you can actually begin your floral business, determine exactly what type you want to start. A retail florist business allows you to serve customers and complete floral arrangements. However, you could opt to start a wholesale business that is responsible for growing flowers and providing them to retail stores. Remember that flower buying in the UK can fluctuate according to special occasions. Therefore, you will need to estimate your expected level of demand so that you can work out how much stock to buy.

It is essential that you provide proper care of your flowers and plants, and it is important that you have all the equipment and supplies necessary. A retail business requires a cooler to keep cut flowers from wilting too fast, while a wholesale business should have a greenhouse or other optimal growing space. Most florists have a main retail area, a preparation area and storeroom with refrigeration. Examine what you need in advance and budget accordingly.

The most commonly made mistake by those starting a small floral business is the failure to specialise. Having a broad appeal will win over a larger population but without a specific profile you may prevent customers from considering your business. You might choose to supply weddings, funerals, official occasions, holiday displays or even allergen-free artificial flower creations. There is a range of products you can offer depending on your niche, including pot and bedding plants, vegetable seeds and bulbs, pots and vases, custom-made bouquets, ready-made arrangements, flower care products, greeting cards, seasonal Christmas trees and decorations, and red roses for Valentine's Day.

Check out floral wholesalers and open accounts with them. If it is possible to eliminate the middle man (the wholesaler) and buy direct from local growers, your raw materials will be cheaper. Compare other local florists' flower arrangement prices similar to those you wish to sell and then prepare your price list. You will not only face competition from supermarkets, but convenience stores, fruit and veg shops, nurseries, garden centres, petrol stations and online shops as well. Keep your prices in the general region of those set by your competition, if you can do so without making a loss.

A worthwhile online resource to keep in touch with is Master Florist (www.masterflorist.com). The British Florist Association (BFA, www.britishflorist association.org) represents all those in the floristry sector.

The Flowers & Plants Association (www.flowers.org) is the UK's promotional organisation for all cut flowers and indoor plants, no matter where they are grown or where they are sold. It is funded by its membership, which includes companies from right across the floriculture industry – growers and breeders who produce the plants; wholesalers and importers who find the right growers in the right countries; retailers of all kinds including designer florists, high street outlets, market stalls, online retailers and supermarkets; floristry schools and colleges; and associated companies like accessories suppliers. Staff are experienced in all aspects of PR but their unique selling point is their knowledge of the industry.

Alarm Bell

Creating lovely floral arrangements is only one part of the job. Make sure you don't get bogged down in a quagmire of paperwork, flowers to condition, buckets to scrub and staff to look after. Keep your shop well stocked and running efficiently and you will get running orders.

Opening a health shop

There are more than 1,000 health food stores in the UK, according to the National Association of Health Stores (NAHS). A health food shop is a one-stop shop for wholefoods, organics, allergy-free foods, vitamins, minerals, herbs, amino acids, sports nutrition, essential fatty acids, cruelty-free bodycare, environmentally-friendly household cleaners and recycled paper products.

The very first British health food store was opened by James Henry Cook in Corporation Street, Birmingham, in 1898. Originally called the Vegetarian Food Depot its name was quickly changed to Pitman's Health Food Store after a customer enquired which foods would help her particular medical condition and James Henry Cook realised he was selling foods for health. The building, which still stands today, also housed a seven-storey vegetarian hotel and vegetarian restaurant and was named after Sir Isaac Pitman, who gave us the shorthand system and was a notable vegetarian of the time.

During the early 1900s, many health food shops followed, initially in the cities and then the major towns. In London, pioneer names such as Eustace Miles, William G. Orr and Edgar Saxon opened health food stores in Chandos Street, Ludgate Hill and Wigmore Street respectively. Shearns of Tottenham Court Road was a veritable health food mecca. The Martin family opened the Savoy Health Store in Nottingham, which passed through three generations of the same family. William Orr had expanded to four shops, his others being in the UK capitals of Belfast, Cardiff and Glasgow.

A JOURNEY TO BETTER HEALTH

By 1925 there were a few hundred health food stores in the UK. More were added steadily throughout the next decades. In 1920, Samuel Ryder started Heath and Heather: The Herb Specialists in St Albans. His name will long be remembered as the presenter of the Ryder Cup golf trophy. From one shop in St Albans, his family business expanded to 45 health food stores by the 1960s. The Heath and Heather chain was eventually bought out in 1968 and merged with some 30 Realfood shops, re-named Holland & Barrett. Today the company has 500 health food shops in towns all over the UK.

During the war and the continuing rationing period, health stores had a particular part to play. They were a source of veggie protein sustenance on which the nation's vegetarians could rely. Despite the shipping casualties most stores enjoyed a smooth supply of nuts and nutmeat products.

The 1960s witnessed dynamic growth in health foods and the number of stores increased to more than 2,000 along with health food departments in department stores such as Harrods and Selfridges. Although this boom in health foods led to some big companies setting up shop, the market was still dominated by individual entrepreneurs, many with the same altruistic ideals as the early pioneers. It would be described today as 'eating for health' and reversing disease by natural methods.

RISING DEMAND

The success of the health food store message through the latter part of the 20th century also captured the interest of the major food and pharmacy retailers. Despite these challenges, the independent health food store continues to thrive as a result of its ability to adapt and to lead, its infinitely wider range of healthy merchandise and, not least, the expert advice it is able to offer freely to its customers.

Over the past 20 years, the demand for health foods, vitamins and alternative medicines has risen rapidly. If the natural products industry holds your interest and passion then think about the aspects of owning and running a health food shop. Running a successful store brings an even greater satisfaction, that of knowing you are contributing to the health of society and offering hope to many chronically ill people.

Says NAHS:

> ❮ *Health food stores thrive in the most disparate locations from secondary sites such as market stalls to top shopping malls and even as concessions within top department stores such as Harrods and Selfridges. The success of the store will depend on a number of factors, including demographics. This analysis of the composition of a particular population offers statistics on the age, income, health, politics and the propensity to buy consumer items such as vitamins.* ❯

 Explore other health food stores. Ask suppliers to recommend successful stores for you to visit around the country. Get a feel for what works and what doesn't. Specialist design consultancies servicing the independent store are available for guidance. Don't abandon function for style – high chrome and curved glass may look gorgeous on the computer preview, but may be awkward to merchandise and clean.

CHOOSING YOUR PRODUCTS

Your competition will come from supermarkets, market stalls, convenience stores, delicatessens, retail chemists and other outlets selling vitamins, herbal remedies, diet supplements, homeopathic remedies, cosmetics, green products and organics. Customers are ever more interested in a range of ethical, environmental and health issues so it is a good idea to promote these concerns within your store.

If your planned store is in a busy office community, there is likely to be an opportunity for take-away and ready meals. Your product mix depends on your preference and expertise as well as your demographic. If you wish your store to specialise in body-building products and energy drinks, it makes sense to be close to a number of gyms. Consumers in a health food store are looking for a good range of products, lots of choice and the impression that there is abundance.

Work with your suppliers and ask for their advice – their Top 30 may be a good starting point. Build each brand in store by width rather than depth. If you wish to allocate shelf space for 30 bottles it may make more sense to buy two each of 15 lines, rather than 15 bottles each of two lines. Decide on your product mix, such as food and dietary supplements, vitamins, sports nutrition, herbals, packaged food, fresh takeaways, organics and own label. Most health food shops stock the following.

☐ Bread and cakes.

☐ Butters, jams and spreads.

☐ Cereals and pulses.

☐ Dried fruits.

☐ Fruit and vegetable juices.

☐ Free-range products.

☐ Herbal teas.

☐ Local produce.

☐ Mineral water and energy drinks.

☐ Nuts and seeds.

☐ Non-food health products.

☐ Organic foodstuffs.

☐ Vegetarian and vegan products.

Visit other health food stores. Consider how the multiples choose to display their goods. Think about the layout of your store from a security perspective – where should the information desk and tills be placed to prevent theft? Customer flow and buy-line placement are a fine art, but there are experts available to advise you.

Creating metre-wide bays for each brand and adding ailment category sections limits consumer confusion, streamlines ordering and facilitates good stock management. Nothing sells from the back room, but a good back room may make an excellent consulting room for a practitioner, bringing in rent, customers and creating a knowledgeable atmosphere.

STAFF AND ASSOCIATIONS

Qualified staff are difficult to find in the health food sector. Most people who qualify in complementary therapies tend to then go into practice for themselves. Look for enthusiasm, cleanliness and an ability and willingness to learn. Plenty of training in natural remedies and so on is available within the industry, not always at great cost. What you can't teach is a good attitude. The three key attributes customers look for in a health food store, according to an industry marketing guru, are freshness, range and knowledge.

The trade association serving the health food sector is the National Association of Health Stores (NAHS, www.nahs.co.uk). It started in 1931 to represent the growing number of independent health food stores in the UK. Its aim is to promote to the public the benefits of shopping in locally owned, independent health food stores and to ensure that there is a good standard of customer advice available in all its member stores. It also works with other organisations, such as Consumers for Health Choice (CHC) and the Health Food Manufacturers Association (HFMA), to ensure the maximum possible availability of health food and nutritional products.

HealthNotes (www.nahs.co.uk) is a web-based fully researched and referenced database on ailments and nutritional supplements with interactions and contra-indications. NAHS membership gives you a 10% discount.

Opening a jewellery shop

There was a time when jewellers considered themselves almost a race apart from retailers and certainly nothing to do with the fashion industry. Their businesses had, in general, stayed profitable without exerting much effort. Unlike other sectors of retail, whose very survival depended on continuous innovation, retail jewellers enjoyed a market almost exclusively fed by life's events. Births, deaths, marriages and coming of age all presented sales opportunities, and 'innovation' was not required. Jewellers' share of the nation's discretionary spending was all but assured.

However, with the dismantling of many of life's traditions, the invention of new gadgets and experiences on which customers could spend their cash, and new routes to market such as TV shopping and the internet that bypassed the retailer, jewellers found themselves with a fight on their hands. Fresh ideas were required. And while the multiple jewellers have played their part in supplying them, independents, who still take more than 20% of sales of precious and gemstone jewellery, have really made the running in the race to innovate.

Therefore, the challenge over the last five or six years has been to vastly improve visual merchandising by sweeping away the dusty, pad-filled windows of yesteryear, to identify and relentlessly entice target audiences, and to differentiate their business from the mass of jewellers. Abandoning the old 'push' economy and entering the 'pull' market, dragged along by consumer demand, was one of the bitterest pills to swallow. As was the acceptance of brand power.

BRAND AND LIFESTYLE MARKETING

With the exception of premier watch brands, jewellers have been slow to appreciate the positive effect that brands and lifestyle marketing can have on sales. Those that have made the leap have responded by playing on the customer's desire for 'authenticity' and 'meaning' from the jewellery they buy, and have promoted designer identity above all else. Therefore, some customers have become devotees of ranges produced by Paul Spurgeon, Sarah Jordan, Stephen Webster and the like, while others' passion is fuelled by such collectables as troll beads.

Today's most successful jewellers have freed themselves from the limiting preconceptions passed down from previous generations and taken a fresh look at the business of selling jewellery. They have responded to the individual desires of their customers through bespoke work and have mirrored their customers' lifestyle aspirations. Only in this way have they secured themselves a place in their clients' minds. Other jewellers have taken that process one stage further by becoming the brand, and have assured themselves a healthier profit margin by designing and manufacturing their own ranges and controlling the means of production.

So much for the theory then. How do you make it happen? As with all businesses, it boils down to having the right strategy; understanding your market, then beating the competition. Simple, I hear you say, 'but surely there must be more to it than that?' And the answer is 'not really'. The theory of retailing (explained elsewhere in this book) applies just as well to jewellery as it does to fashion or any other product, except unlike clothes, food and other commodities, buying jewellery is almost entirely discretionary. Jewellers are harnessing the emotive power that comes from customers' desire to possess something that is beautiful and has intrinsic value.

DEFINING YOUR MARKET

So what are the practical things a budding jeweller should look out for? As with all retailers, location is key, and, unless your trading plans and finance allow for heavy advertising spending on becoming a destination, then you need a prominent location.

Second is a good idea and a clear understanding of your target market. Fashion retailers have been good at defining target markets by age, gender, social standing and so on, and building their brand image around that. Historically, jewellers have not. So define your market and build your brand image around it and stick to it. But to do that you need appropriate stock, so do your research at trade shows and exhibitions, calculate your budgets and buy sensibly – financing dead stock and buying errors are the main cause of cash flow difficulties.

Lastly, and by no means least, get yourself trained. I cannot over-emphasise how important it is to develop real professionalism. After all is said and done, and after all the changes of recent years, being a jeweller is still a position of trust and you owe it to your customers to be as knowledgeable about your product as possible. There is a lot to learn.

The above section on Opening a Jewellery Shop has been provided by Michael Hoare, Chief Executive, The National Association of Goldsmiths, www.jewellers-online.org

A FEW OTHER POINTERS

According to government statistics, households in the UK spend about £100 a year on personal effects, including jewellery. Start by deciding on the type of items you will sell and the services you will offer. These could include: antique jewellery; diamond, pearl and gem settings; watches and clocks; fashion jewellery; or more expensive pieces. You could also offer items, alterations, repairs, valuations, engraving or a pawnbroking service.

More expensive merchandise will be bought by older customers, while the younger generation may opt for cheaper fashion jewellery. Your main competition will come from online retailers, department stores, mail order companies and even craft fairs. It may be difficult to match their prices so maybe you should think about specialising in a particular form of jewellery.

TRAINING

The National Association of Goldsmiths (NAG, www.jewellers-online.org) represents jewellery retailers in the UK and offers training courses. Termed JET (Jewellery Education and Training), these courses cover a range of topics from basic product and selling-skills knowledge through to management and valuation expertise.

The Professional Jewellers' Diploma (JET 1) is studied over a maximum period of six months and students can enrol at any time of year. Course topics include sales techniques and customer service, jewellery product knowledge, precious metals and hallmarks, watches and clocks, silverware and gifts, anniversaries, types of chains, birthstones, carat sizes and diamond shapes.

The Professional Jewellers' Diploma (JET 2) is studied over a period of 12 months. Students who have the JET 1 certificate are eligible to enrol in JET 2 during January, February or March, as well as during August, September and October. JET 2 takes a more in-depth look at the subjects covered in JET 1 such as security, hallmarks and gemstones (including diamond treatments and stimulants). Other subjects include the history of jewellery, modern designers, display, principles of valuations, service and repairs, consumer law and consumer confidence.

JET 1 and 2 have become the benchmark for retail jewellers' staff. The courses, studied over an 18-month period, are designed to provide first-class product knowledge and a wide ranging understanding of the trade, including design, manufacture, hallmarking, gemstones, silverware, horology, antiques, legal matters, repair handling, selling techniques and window displays. Holders of the diploma may use the initials PJ Dip after their name.

The Professional Jewellers' Gemstone Diploma provides those in the industry with an understanding of the appearance, properties and major features of the gemstones they are most likely to encounter in the business. The course focuses on the needs of the industry and the bias is thus towards understanding and selling more than science. The course is a home-study training medium, and is studied over a maximum period of 12 months. The principal aims of the course are to enable jewellers to:

- □ converse knowledgeably and interestingly with their customers;
- □ use and understand correct terminology;
- □ advise customers about the suitability and care of gems;
- □ understand and be able to explain what affects 'quality' and thus value;
- □ have an understanding of birth and anniversary gemstones, history and the various myths that can add interest to a gem;
- □ understand and carry out essential testing procedures to indicate the identity of gemstones and to help distinguish between natural, synthetic and imitation gemstones.

The Professional Jewellers' Management Diploma is tailored for the needs of proprietors and senior staff and is designed to promote an efficient and profitable business. Success in retail jewellery management depends on developing skills in organisational, personal and people management. Topics covered include appraisal techniques, customer care strategy, handling complaints, leadership and motivation, recruitment and interviewing, delegation and team building.

The Professional Jewellers' Valuation Diploma course provides an opportunity to learn about the practice and science of valuing. Jewellery valuations require expertise and discipline in order to ensure that descriptions are precise, identifications correct and measurements accurate. However, valuing is not an exact science – descriptions and value can be a matter of opinion, as can choices relating to valuing methodologies.

Other sector snippets

OFFICE PRODUCTS AND STATIONERY SHOP

It is reported that the office goods retailing sector is worth about £5 billion in the UK. There are currently about 2,500 to 3,000 office product dealers in the UK, with 40% having glass-fronted retail outlets. The main operator is Staples. There are also a number of online retailers, such as Mr Office and Viking Direct. Traditionally, the market consisted only of stationery products such as envelopes, office paper, writing instruments, filing supplies and desktop accessories. In the early 1990s, office furniture, presentation and planning supplies, and electronic office supplies were added. Recently, PCs, printers, audio-visual projectors, shredders, binders, laminators, arts and graphic supplies have been added to the pantheon.

Key sector trends show:

- ☐ a decline in envelope sales due to the slow down in postal traffic as consumers switch to emailing and e-invoicing;
- ☐ a fairly static demand for books and pads;
- ☐ a varying demand for cut office paper, with copier paper, letterhead, offset and duplicator paper showing a decline and specialist coated inkjet paper increasing at a slower rate;
- ☐ a mature writing and graphic supplies market;
- ☐ a slight decline in storage and filing products;
- ☐ the former rapid growth in electronic office supplies is now slowing down;
- ☐ a mature market in office and desk accessories with volume demand driven by office employment;
- ☐ a healthy presentation and planning market driven by business presentations;
- ☐ a collapse in office furniture driven by gross domestic product (GDP) and business confidence.

If you believe there is a niche for a small, independent stationery store in your area offering products that consumers demand, at a good price, then you should speak to the British Office Supplies & Services (BOSS) Federation (www.bossfederation.co.uk). This is the trade association serving the UK office products industry, including stationery, office machines and supplies, office furniture, office systems and related product areas.

TOY SHOP

According to government statistics, households (with and without children) in the UK spend about £105 a year on toys, games and hobbies. However, competition is fierce in this sector, with large stores such as Toys R Us, Argos, supermarkets, market stalls and a variety of other retailers all selling toys.

The Toy Retailers Association (TRA, www.toyretailersassociation.co.uk) categorises toys as ranging from rattles, squeaky toys and balls for babies (0–12 months); pull-along toys, dolls, finger paints, soft toys and crayons for toddlers (1–3 years); construction kits, train sets and puzzles for pre-school children (3–5 years); and bat and ball games, pencil sets, colouring sets, craft and hobby kits and musical instruments for children of school age (5 years and upwards). Action figures, play-sets, games and collectables as well as radio-controlled and outdoor toys add to the excitement for older children. Children aged two to three receive the most toys but expenditure focuses around the six to eight-year-olds.

TRA says that the current trend in all sectors of the market is towards electronic toys and computer-assisted learning, with many of these highly developed to attract children. These fully developed toys are no longer the preserve of electronic and computer game traders and independent toy retailers need to understand the market. Sales of traditional toys and games have been relatively static over the last ten years in real terms.

Fashionable trends

The popularity of toys also follows film and TV trends with licenses launching spin-off merchandise. The growing cable and satellite television markets are likely to further contribute to this. Licensing is particularly important as demonstrated by the success of the many top-selling toys. However, with fashion trends it is often difficult to predict what will be popular and toy retailers can be left with a backlog of unwanted stock. Toy retailers must also compete with other sectors including fashion, sport, music and entertainment for leisure expenditure.

 Regardless of the type of toy shop you choose, most types experience similar trading patterns: around 15% per quarter until the pre-Christmas period when you take around 55% of your turnover. Margins are dictated by the type of product, but you should strive for around 40%.

The National Association of Toy and Leisure Libraries (www.natll.org.uk) runs one-day and three-day courses on learning through play, toy and play workshops, and introducing board games. For more information on opening a toy shop, contact the Association of Toy Retailers (www.associationoftoyretailers.co.uk) and, for a list of suppliers, speak to the British Toy & Hobby Association (www.btha.co.uk). The British Toymakers Guild (www.toymakersguild.co.uk) provides information on hand-crafted and wooden toys.

FAIRTRADE SHOPS

Ethical products that help producers in developing countries have seen an increase in recent years. Fairtrade certified products in the UK have grown by 50% a year. Fairtrade guarantees a fair deal for disadvantaged producers by making sure they receive a fair price for their work and goods. Fairtrade items are generally slightly more expensive than similar products, but more and more people are happy to pay a little extra to help Third World producers become self-sufficient. All fairtrade products are marked with the easy-to-recognise Fairtrade Mark.

Fairtrade certifies Third World producers and pays them a set minimum price for their goods, intended to cover production costs and give them a living wage. In return, fairtrade producers must meet certain standards. For most products the standards set a fairtrade minimum price that covers the costs of sustainable production. These are set by the Fairtrade Labelling Organisation (FLO) International. Only licensees, such as importers and manufacturers, that are registered with the Fairtrade Foundation can apply the Fairtrade Mark to a product.

You will probably buy your fairtrade goods either directly from manufacturers or importers, or from registered wholesalers in the UK. The Fairtrade Foundation website (www.fairtrade.org.uk) has a list of wholesalers that sell fairtrade marked products to retailers in the UK.

When you buy fairtrade goods from a wholesaler or registered manufacturer, you should expect to pay a little more than you normally would for similar products. Although fairtrade prices are higher, you can probably charge your customers a little bit more for them without rocking the boat. The Fairtrade Foundation is not involved in setting retail prices, so your mark-up is entirely up to you. Offering fairtrade products can be an appealing selling point for your shop and can help to attract ethically aware customers.

The Fairtrade Foundation will provide useful materials and advice to help you to advertise your fairtrade ranges. Any promotional materials that contain the Fairtrade Mark, such as posters or leaflets, must be approved by the Foundation. The 'Manual for Promotional Materials' contains full guidance on how the Fairtrade Mark should be used. You can download it from the Fairtrade Foundation at www.fairtrade.org.uk. The Fairtrade Foundation also organises a Fairtrade Fortnight each year to promote the system.

Dos and don'ts

Finally, the important dos and don'ts from Amanda Hartley of Amanda's Blue Orchid Florist in Hull, who is also Hull's 2009 Young Entrepreneur of the Year:

Do: Go for it.

Do: Get the right training.

Do: Use all your contacts in the media, such as free paper reports and free advertising on the radio. Even call in and request a song, it gets your name out there!

Do: Speak to Business Link and any other relevant organisations (in my case Youth Enterprise).

Don't: Always listen to other people – trust in yourself.

Don't: Follow other businesses – have your own style and a product that's unique.

Don't: Put too much money into it – have a 'pull-out' clause.

Don't: Be scared to give something a go.

USEFUL ORGANISATIONS

National organisations

Acas (Advisory, Conciliation & Arbitration Service), Brandon House, 180 Borough High Street, London SE1 1LW; tel 020 7210 3613, helpline 0845 747 4747; www.acas.org.uk; 13 regional offices

Association of British Insurers (ABI), 51 Gresham Street, London EC2V 7HQ; tel 020 7600 3333; www.abi.org.uk

Association of Chartered Accountants (ACCA), 29 Lincoln's Inns Field, London WC2A 3EE; tel 020 7059 5000; email info@accaglobal.com; www.accaglobal.com

British Association for Fair Trade Shops, 9 Thames Street, Charlbury, Oxford OX7 3QL; tel 078 6675 9201; email info@bafts.org.uk; www.bafts.org.uk

The British Chambers of Commerce (BCC) is an association of the main Chambers of Commerce found in each region of the UK. Each Chamber is a separate membership organisation and services provided can vary with each Chamber. Businesses of all sizes may join their local Chamber on payment of the relevant annual membership fee. A list of Chambers can be obtained from BCC, 65 Petty France, London SW1H 9EU; tel 020 7654 5800; email info@britishchambers.org.uk; www.britishchambers.org.uk

British Franchise Association, A2 Danebrook Court, Oxford Office Village, Langford Lane, Oxford OX5 1LQ; tel 01865 379 892; www.thebfa.org

British Insurance Brokers' Association, 4 Bevis Marks, London EC3A 7NT; tel 0870 950 1790; email enquiries@biba.org.uk; www.biba.org.uk

The Chartered Institute of Marketing, Moor Hall, Cookham, Maidenhead, Berkshire SL6 9QH; tel 01628 427 500; www.cim.co.uk

Chartered Institute of Personnel and Development (CIPD), 151 The Broadway, London SW19 1JQ; tel 020 8612 6200

CIC Regulator, CIC Team, Room 3.68, Companies House, Crown Way, Mandy, Cardiff CF14 3UZ; tel 029 2034 6228; email cicregulator@companieshouse.gov.uk; www.cicregulator.gov.uk

Confederation of British Industry (CBI), 103 New Oxford Street, London WC1A 1DU; tel 020 7379 7400; www.cbi.org.uk

Companies House, Crown Way, Cardiff CF14 3UZ; tel 0303 1234 500; email enquiries@companies-house.gov.uk; www.companieshouse.gov.uk; offices in London and Edinburgh

Department for Business, Innovation and Skills (BIS), 1 Victoria Street, London SW1H 0ET; tel 020 7215 5000; email enquiries@bis.gsi.gov.uk; www.bis.gov.uk

Entrepreneurial Exchange, Barncluith Business Centre, Townhead Street, Hamilton ML3 7DP; tel 01698 285 650; email info@entrepreneurial-exchange.co.uk; www.entrepreneurial-exchange.co.uk

The Fairtrade Foundation, Room 204, 16 Baldwin's Gardens, London EC1N 7RJ; www.fairtrade.org.uk; part of the international fairtrade movement and oversees all aspects of fairtrade in the UK

Federation of Small Businesses (FSB), Sir Frank Whittle Way, Blackpool Business Park, Blackpool FY4 2FE; tel 01253 336 000; email ho@fsb.co.uk; www.fsb.co.uk

Finance and Leasing Association (FLA), 2nd Floor, Imperial House, 15–19 Kingsway, London WC2B 6UN; tel 020 7836 6511; email info@fla.org.uk; www.fla.org.uk

Financial Ombudsman Service (FOS), South Quay Plaza, 183 Marsh Wall, London E14 9SR; tel 0845 080 1800; www.financial-ombudsman.org.uk

Financial Services Authority (FSA), 25 The North Colonnade, Canary Wharf, London E14 5HS; tel 020 7066 1000, helpline 0845 606 1234; www.fsa.gov.uk

Forum of Private Business, Ruskin Chambers, Drury Lane, Knutsford WA16 6HA; tel 01565 634 467; email info@fpb.org; www.fpb.co.uk

Franchise Development Services (FDS), Franchise House, 56 Surrey Street, Norwich NR1 3FD; tel 01603 620 301; email enquiries@fdsltd.com; www.fdsfranchise.com

Health and Safety Executive, Rose Court, 2 Southwark Bridge, London SE1 9HS; tel 0845 345 0055; www.hse.gov.uk

HM Revenue & Customs (HMRC); tel 0845 915 4515; www.hmrc.gov.uk

ICS Ltd, Clydeway Centre, Skypark 5, 1st Floor, 45 Finnieston Street, Glasgow G3 8JU; tel 0141 302 5487; email icscourseadvisors@ics-uk.co.uk; www.icslearn.co.uk

Information Commissioner's Office, Wycliffe House, Water Lane, Wilmslow, Cheshire SK9 5AF; tel 084 630 6060 or 01625 545 745; www.ico.gov.uk; offices in Scotland, Wales and Northern Ireland

The Institute of Chartered Accountants in England and Wales (ICAEW), PO Box 433, Chartered Accountants Hall, Moorgate Place, London EC2P 2BJ; tel 020 7920 8100; www.icaew.co.uk

The Institute of Chartered Accounts of Scotland (ICAS), CA House, 21 Haymarket Yards, Edinburgh EH12 5BH; tel 0131 347 0100; www.icas.org.uk

Institute of Credit Management, The Water Mill, Station Road, South Luffenham, Leicestershire LE15 8NB; tel 01780 722 900; email info@icm.org.uk; www.icm.org.uk

Institute of Grocery Distribution (IGD), Grange Lane, Letchmore Heath, Watford, Hertfordshire WD25 8GD; www.igd.com; produces a huge range of publications covering all aspects of the UK food and grocery industry

Institute of Insurance Brokers (IIB), Higham Business Centre, Midland Road, Higham Ferrers, Northamptonshire NN10 8DW; tel 01933 410 003; www.iib-uk.com

The Law Society, 113 Chancery Lane, London WC2A 1PL; Find a solicitor service: tel 0870 606 2555; www.lawsociety.org.uk

learndirect, Dearing House, Young Street, Sheffield S1 4UP; tel 0800 101 901; www.learndirect.co.uk

National Federation of Enterprise Agencies (NFEA), 12 Stephenson Court, Fraser Road, Priory Business Park, Bedford MK44 3WJ; tel 01234 831 623, email enquiries@nfea.com; www.nfea.com. A membership body for Local Enterprise Agencies, offering a comprehensive range of services to pre-start, start-up and micro businesses. It also runs the Small Business Advice Service (SBAS) which provides an internet-based advice service for entrepreneurs, owner managers and the self-employed; www.smallbusinessadvice.org.uk

Office for National Statistics, Room 1.015, Government Buildings, Cardiff Road, Newport NP10 8XG; tel 0845 601 3034; email info@statistics.gov.uk; www.statistics.gov.uk

Oxford Institute of Retail Management, Said Business School, University of Oxford, Park End Street, Oxford OX1 1HP; tel 01865 288 800; www.sbs.ox.ac.uk

Prince's Initiative for Mature Enterprise (PRIME), Astral House, 1268 London Road, London SW16 4ER; tel 0800 783 1904; email prime@ace.org.uk; www.primeinitiative.org.uk

The Small Business Bureau, Curzon House, Church Road, Windlesham, Surrey GU20 6BH; tel 01276 452 010; www.smallbusinessbureau.org.uk

Trading Standards Institute, 1 Sylvan Court, Sylvan Way, Southfields Business Park, Basildon, Essex SS15 6TH; tel 0845 608 9400; email institute@tsi.org.uk; www.tradingstandards.gov.uk

Valuation Office Agency (VOA), New Court, 48 Carey Street, London WC2A 2JE; tel 020 7506 1700 or 0845 602 1507 to speak directly with the office closest to you; www.voa.gov.uk

WiRE (Women in Rural Enterprise), Harper Adams University College, Edgmond, Newport, Shropshire TF10 8NB; tel 01952 815 338; email info@wireuk.org; www.wireuk.org. Offers business support to women in rural business.

Regional development agencies

Advantage West Midlands, 3 Priestley Wharf, Holt Street, Aston Science Park, Birmingham B7 4BN; tel 0121 380 3500; www.advantagewm.co.uk

East of England Development Agency (EEDA), The Business Centre, Station Road, Histon CB24 9LQ; tel 01223 713 900; www.eeda.org.uk

East Midlands Development Agency (EMDA), Apex Court, City Link, Nottingham NG2 4LA; tel 0115 988 8300; www.emda.org.uk

London Development Agency (LDA), Palestra, 197 Blackfriars Road, London SE1 8AA; tel 020 7593 8000; www.lda.gov.uk

Northwest Regional Development Agency (NWDA), PO Box 37, Renaissance House, Centre Park, Warrington, Cheshire WA1 1XB; tel 01925 400 100; www.nwda.co.uk.

One North East, Riverside House, Goldcrest Way, Newburn Riverside, Newcastle NE15 8NY; tel 0191 229 6200; www.onenortheast.co.uk

South East England Development Agency (SEEDA), Cross Lanes, Guildford GU1 1YA; tel 01483 484 200; www.seeda.co.uk

South West of England Regional Development Agency, Sterling House, Dix's Field, Exeter, Devon EX1 1QA; tel 01392 214 747; www.southwestrda.org.uk

Yorkshire Forward, Victoria House, 2 Victoria Place, Holbeck, Leeds LS11 5AE; tel 0113 394 9600; www.yorkshire-forward.com

Websites

Business Link (England)
tel 0845 600 9006
www.businesslink.gov.uk

Business Eye (Wales)
tel 0845 796 9798
www.businesseye.org.uk

Business Gateway (Scotland)
tel 0845 609 6611
www.bgateway.com

Invest Northern Ireland
tel 028 9023 9090
www.investni.com

Scottish Enterprise
tel 0845 607 8787
www.scottish-enterprise.com

Workspace (Northern Ireland)
tel 028 7962 8113
www.workspace.org.uk

Trade Associations

Angling Trades Association (ATA), Federation House, Stoneleigh Park, Warwickshire CV8 2RF; tel 024 7641 4999 ext 204; email ata@sportsandplay.com; www.anglingtradesassociation.com

Angling Trust, Eastwood House, 6 Rainbow Street, Leominster, Herefordshire HR6 8DQ; tel 0844 770 0616; email admin@anglingtrust.net; www.anglingtrust.net

Association of Convenience Stores (ACS), 17 Farnborough Street, Farnborough GU14 8AG; tel 01252 515 001; www.thelocalshop.com

Association of Cycle Traders (ACT), PO Box 5110, Hove BN52 9EB; tel 0870 428 8404; email info@actsmart.biz; www.actsmart.biz/cycles

The Booksellers Association, Minster House, 272 Vauxhall Bridge Road, London SW1V 1BA; tel 020 7802 0802; email mail@booksellers.org.uk; www.booksellers.org.uk

The British Antique Dealers' Association, 20 Rutland Gate, London SW7 1BD; tel 020
    7589 4128; www.bada.org
British Association for Fair Trade Shops, 9 Thames Street, Charlbury, Oxford OX7 3QL;
    tel 078 6675 9201; email info@bafts.org.uk; www.bafts.org.uk.
British Clothing Industry Association (BCIA), 5 Portland Place, London W1B 1PW; tel
    020 7636 7788; email contact@5portlandplace.org.uk; www.5portlandplace.org.uk
British Florist Association (BFA), PO Box 5161, Dudley, West Midlands DY1 9FX; tel
    0844 800 7299; email info@britishfloristassociation.org; www.britishflorist
    association.org
British Hardware Federation (BHF), 225 Bristol Road, Edgbaston, Birmingham B5 7UB;
    tel 0121 446 6688; email info@bhfgroup.co.uk; www.bhfgroup.co.uk
Bridal Industry Suppliers Association; tel 01992 621 912; info@bisassociation.co.uk;
    www.bisassociation.co.uk
British Office Supplies & Services Federation (BOSS), Farringdon Point, 2935 Farringdon
    Road, London EC1M 3JF; tel 0845 450 1565; email info@bossfederation.co.uk;
    www.bossfederation.com
British Retail Consortium (BRC), 21 Dartmouth Street, London SW1H 9BP; tel 020 7854
    8900; www.brc.org.uk. This is the lead trade association representing the whole range of
    retailers, including independents, selling a wide range of products through centre of
    town, out of town, rural and virtual stores.
British Shops and Stores Association Limited, Middleton House, 2 Main Road, Middleton
    Cheney, Banbury, Oxfordshire OX17 2TN; tel 01295 712 277; www.british-
    shops.co.uk
British Toy & Hobby Association, 80 Camberwell Road, London SE5 0EG; tel 020 7701
    7271; email queries@btha.co.uk; www.btha.co.uk
Crafts Council, 44a Pentonville Road, Islington, London N1 9BY; tel 020 7806 2500;
    www.craftscouncil.org.uk
Fine Art Trade Guild, 16-18 Empress Place, London SW6 1TT; tel 020 7381 6616;
    www.fineart.co.uk
Federation of Communications Services (FCS), Provident House, Burrell Row,
    Beckenham, Kent BR3 1AT; tel 020-8249 6363; www.fcs.org.uk
Federation of Sports and Play Associations (FSPA), Federation House, Stoneleigh Park,
    Warwickshire CV8 2RF; tel 024 7641 4999; email admin@sportsandplay.com;
    www.sportsandplay.com
Flowers & Plants Association, 266270 Flower Market, New Covent Garden Market,
    London SW8 5NB; tel 020 7738 8044; email info@flowers.org.uk; www.flowers.org.uk
Fresh Produce Consortium, Minerva House, Minerva Business Park, Lynch Wood,
    Peterborough PE2 6FT; tel 01733 237 117; www.freshproduce.org.uk
Furniture Industry Research Association (FIRA), Maxwell Road, Stevenage, Hertfordshire
    SG1 2EW; tel 01438 777 700; email info@fira.co.uk; www.fira.co.uk
The Guild of Fine Food, Guild House, Station Road, Wincanton, Somerset BA9 9FE, tel
    01963 824 464, www.finefoodworld.co.uk

Horticultural Trades Association (HTA), Horticulture House, 19 High Street, Theale, Reading RG7 5AH; tel 0118 930 3132; email info@the-hta.org.uk; www.the-hta.org.uk

Independent Footwear Retailers Association, PO Box 123, Banbury, Oxfordshire OX15 6WB; tel 01295 738 726; email ifra@shoeshop.org.uk; www.shoeshop.org.uk

Intellect UK, Russell Square House, 1012 Russell Square, London WC1B 5EE; tel 020 7331 2000; www.intellectuk.org

Knitting & Crochet Guild, Unit 4, Lee Mills, Scholes, Holmfirth HD9 1RJ; email info@knitting-and-crochet-guild.org.uk; www.knitting-and-crochet-guild.org.uk.

Master Florist, 68 First Avenue, Mortlake, London SW14 8SR; tel 020 8939 6474; www.masterflorist.com

National Association of Goldsmiths, 78a Luke Street, London EC2A 4XG; tel 020 7613 4445; www.jewellers-online.org

National Association of Health Stores, PO Box 14177, Tranent EH34 5WX; tel 01875 341 408; email nahsoffice@gmail.com; www.nahs.co.uk

National Association of Specialist Computer Retailers (NASCR), c/o 13 New Street, Louth, Lincolnshire LN11 9PT; tel 0845 644 0715; www.nascr.net

National Farmers' Retail & Markets Association, 12 Southgate Street, Winchester, Hampshire SO23 9EF; tel 0845 458 8420; email info@farma.org.uk; www.farma.org.uk

National Federation of Retail Newsagents (NFRN), Yeoman House, Sekforde Street, London EC1R 0HF; tel 020 7253 4225, email service@nfrnonline.com, www.nfrnonline.com

Outdoor Industries Association; www.outdoorindustriesassociation.co.uk

Radio, Electrical and Television Retailers' Association (RETRA), Retra House, St John's Terrace, 1 Ampthill Street, Bedford MK42 9EY; tel 01234 269 110; email retra@retra.co.uk; www.retra.co.uk

Retail Bridalwear Association, 106 Broad Street Mall, Reading RG1 7QA; tel 01494 445155; email rbaltd@fsmail.net; www.weddingshops.org

Rural Crafts Association, Heights Cottage, Brook Road, Wormley, Godalming, Surrey GU8 5UA; tel 01428 682 292; www.ruralcraftsassociation.co.uk

Rural Shops Alliance, Egdon Hall, Lynch Lane, Weymouth, Dorset DT4 9DN; tel 01305 752 044; email info@rural-shops-alliance.co.uk; www.rural-shops-alliance.co.uk

Toy Retailers Association, 207 Mercury House, Willoughton Drive, Foxby Lane Business Park, Gainsborough, Lincolnshire DN21 1DY; tel 0870 753 7437; email enquiries@toyretailerassociation.co.uk; www.toyretailerassociation.co.uk

FURTHER READING

Antiques Trade Gazette, 115 Shaftesbury Avenue, London WC2H 8AF; tel 020 7420 6600; email info@antiquestradegazette.com; www.antiquestradegazette.com. Weekly newspaper, £45 a year

Art Business Today, Fine Art Trade Guild, 1618 Empress Place, London SW6 1TT; tel 020 7381 6616; www.fineart.co.uk. Monthly, £26 a year

BikeBiz, Intent Media Ltd, Saxon House, 6a St Andrews Street, Hertford, Hertfordshire SG14 1JA; tel 01580 883 848; www.bikebiz.com. Monthly magazine, £50 for 12 issues

Bridal Buyer, 1 Canada Square, Canary Wharf, London E14 5AP; tel 020 7772 8317; www.bridalbuyer.com. Bi-monthly

Carpet & Flooring Review, Gearing Media Group, 4 Red Barn Mews, High Street, Battle, East Sussex TN33 0AG; tel 01424 774 982; email info@gearingmediagroup.com; www.cfr-magazine.com. Monthly magazine, £75 a year

Craftbusiness, Aceville Publications, 25 Phoenix Court, Hawkins Road, Colchester, Essex CO2 8JY; tel 01206 505 983; www.craftbusiness.com

DIY Week, Faversham House Group Ltd, 232a Addington Road, South Croydon, Surrey CR2 8UZ; tel 020 8651 7148; www.diyweek.net. Weekly magazine, £102 a year

Drapers, Greater London House, Hampstead Road, London NW1 7EJ; tel 020 7728 5000; www.drapersonline.com. Weekly fashion magazine, £225 a year

Electrical Retail News (ERT), Taylist Media, 4th Floor, Equitable House, Harrow HA1 2EW; tel 020 8515 6880; www.ertonline.co.uk. 26 issues a year, £98.40

Fine Food Digest, The Guild of Fine Food, Guild House, Station Road, Wincanton, Somerset BA9 9FE; tel 01963 824 464; www.finefoodworld.co.uk. 10 issues a year, £40

Fresh Produce Journal (FPJ), Lockwood Press, 1 Nine Elms Lane, London SW8 5NN; tel 020 7501 0300; email info@fpj.co.uk; www.freshinfo.com. Weekly, £125 a year

Healthmatters, OLM-Pavilion, Richmond House, Richmond Road, Brighton, East Sussex BN2 3RL; tel 0844 880 5061; email info@pavpub.com; www.pavpub.com. Quarterly magazine, £65 a year

Health Food Business, Target Publishing, The Old Dairy, Hudsons Farm, Fieldgate Lane, Ugley Green, Essex CM22 6HJ; tel 01279 810 088; www.healthfoodbusiness.co.uk. Monthly magazine, £54

The Independent, Association of Cycle Traders, PO Box 5110, Hove, Sussex BN52 9EB; tel 0870 428 8403; email info@actsmart.biz; www.thecyclingexperts.co.uk. Quarterly journal for bicycle retailers

Independent Electrical Retailers (IER), Dateam Publishing Ltd, 15a London Road, Maidstone, Kent ME16 8LY; tel 01622 687 031; www.independent electricalretailer.co.uk

Independent Retail News, Metropolis Business Publishing, 6th Floor, Davis House, 2 Robert Street, Croydon CR0 1QQ; www.talkingretail.com. Fortnightly, £115 a year

The Jeweller, The National Association of Goldsmiths, 78a Luke Street, London EC2A 4XG; tel 020 7613 4445; www.jewellers-online.org. Bi-monthly magazine, £45 for six issues

Lingerie Buyer, Hemming Group, 32 Vauxhall Bridge Road, London SW1V 2SS; tel 020 7973 6694; email customer@hgluk.com; www.lingerie-buyer.co.uk. Eight issues a year, £75

Mobile, Noble House Media, 1416 Pulteney Street, London W1F 9ND; tel 020 7440 3823; www.mobiletoday.co.uk. Weekly, £115 a year

Natural Products and Organic Products, Diversified Business Communications UK, Blenheim House, 119120 Church Street, Brighton, East Sussex BN1 1UD; tel 01273 645 116; www.naturalproductsonline.co.uk. Eleven issues a year, £59

Organic & Natural Business, Target Publishing, The Old Dairy, Hudsons Farm, Fieldgate Lane, Ugley Green, Essex CM22 6HJ; tel 01279 810 088; www.healthfoodbusiness.co.uk; www.organic-business.com. Six issues a year, £54 for two years

Pet Business World (PBW), 6 The Rickyard, Clifton Reynes, Olney, Buckinghamshire MK46 5LQ; tel 01234 714 644; email info@pbwnews.com; www.pbwnews.com. Monthly, £18 a year

Retail Week, Greater London House, Hampstead Road, London NW1 7EJ; tel 020 7728 5000; www.retail-week.com. Weekly magazine, £245 a year

SGB Sports and Outdoor, SGB Group, Datateam Publishing Ltd, 15a London Road, Maidstone, Kent ME16 8LY; tel 01622 687 031; www.sgb-sports.com

Slipknot, Knitting & Crochet Guild, Unit 4, Lee Mills, Scholes, Holmfirth HD9 1RJ; email info@knitting-and-crochet-guild.org.uk; www.knitting-and-crochet-guild.org.uk

ToyNews, Saxon House, 6a St Andrew Street, Hertford, Hertfordshire SG14 1JA; tel 01992 535 646; www.toynewsmag.com. Monthly trade magazine, £50 for 12 issues

Toys & Playthings, Naishville, 1 Churchgates, The Wilderness, Berkhamstead, Hertfordshire HP4 2AZ; tel 01442 289 930; www.toysnplaythngs.co.uk. Monthly magazine, £65 a year

INDEX

Some other titles from How To Books

START AND RUN A DELICATESSEN
DEBORAH PENRITH

This book will tell you all you need to know to start and run your own delicatessen shop, including choosing the right location; researching your market; writing a business plan and raising finance; how to market your business and attract customers; managing food hygiene and health and safety; how to employ and manage your staff; how to advertise cost effectively; keeping the accounts and handling VAT; and sourcing organic food direct from the farmer, or at markets or trade shows. And once you're up and running it will tell you how to expand your business into other areas such as catering to businesses and private functions and assembling and delivering gift hampers.

ISBN 978-1-84528-314-8

WORK FROM HOME
How to make money working at home – and get the most out of life
JUDY HEMINSLEY

Whether you are planning to run your own business or work from home as an employee for a large company, you will share experiences and be looking for solutions to similar challenges. This is a down-to-earth, practical and friendly guide, designed to help you get the best out of working from home. It includes lots of options to help you choose and develop the arrangements that best suit you and your family. In it you'll discover: whether you and your work are suited to working from home; how to negotiate homeworking with your employer; how to maintain a professional image; how to separate work from home; and much more.

ISBN 978-1-84528-335-3

START AND RUN A SANDWICH AND COFFEE BAR
JILL SUTHERLAND

In this step-by-step guide, the owner of a multi-award winning sandwich and coffee bar tells how you, too, can turn your passion for food into a successful business. Jill Sutherland's comprehensive guide will take you on a stage-by-stage guide to your first year, from idea to opening and then to becoming established. Packed with top tips, real-life examples, checklists and anecdotes, this book provides you with practical and realistic advice from someone who has been there and done it. In it you'll learn how to develop and research your sandwich bar 'idea'; write a professional business plan; find the right shop unit, and fit it out; find and manage suppliers; manage food hygiene, and health and safety; create your menu and source produce; budget, forecast and manage cash flow; launch and generate publicity and employ and manage staff.

ISBN 978-1-84528-333-9

START AND RUN A FISH AND CHIP SHOP OR BURGER BAR
JAMES KAYUI LI

This book offers detailed guidance on how to spot a good location for your premises and how to fit it out. Everything you need to know is here: the advantages and disadvantages of freehold versus a leasehold business; the practice and importance of food hygiene; employing staff, advertising, VAT and book-keeping and even recommended frying and cooking methods.

ISBN 978-1-84528-308-7

BECOME AN APPROVED DRIVING INSTRUCTOR AND SET UP YOUR OWN DRIVING SCHOOL
COLIN CRANE AND PAUL PEARSON

This book is written by two, experienced ADIs (Driving Instructors) who not only run their own, very successful driving schools but are partners in a joint internet business, selling training materials to instructors, trainers and trainees. It is for anyone thinking about becoming a driving instructor, or who is already a trainee instructor, or even for an experienced instructor wanting to set up an independent driving school. You'll discover how to train and to keep training costs to a minimum, how to run your business and how to prepare your clients to pass their driving test.

ISBN 978-1-84528-348-3

START AND RUN A GIFT SHOP
VAL CLARKE

Give yourself and your business a head start by following the advice in this book and making sure your business is built on solid foundations. It will tell you how to research your business idea to ensure it will be a success; what you need to do to turn your idea into reality; and how to manage yourself, your stock and your money to power ahead through good times and bad.

ISBN 978-1-84528-360-5

START AND RUN AN INTERNET BUSINESS
CAROL ANN STRANGE

'An excellent definitive guide.' – *Jobs & Careers*
This book will guide you through the process of establishing a profitable online venture and steer you towards success. You'll learn how to generate online income; create a reliable and appealing virtual shop window; optimise your web venture for growth; generate more profit from affiliate schemes and other prospects and become a successful internet entrepreneur

ISBN 978-1-84528-356-8

HOW TO START AND RUN A PETSITTING BUSINESS
FIONA MCKENZIE

'An absolutely MUST HAVE for anyone who is starting up their own business. The book covers everything you need to know from a person who has gone through it themselves, and is written in a humorous helpful way. A book you will find essential when you are setting up and also to keep, to refer to over the years once your business is up and running.' – *Reader review*

ISBN 978-1-84528-289-9

START & RUN A SUCCESSFUL CLEANING BUSINESS
ROBERT GORDON

This book will give you insider knowledge of the world of office and domestic cleaning and provide you with all the practical tools you need to succeed in a competitive but rewarding industry.

ISBN 978-1-84528-284-4

STARTING & RUNNING A GREETINGS CARD BUSINESS
ELIZABETH WHITE

'Tells the reader everything they need to know about building an exciting and profitable business.' – *Greetings Today*

This book takes you step by step through the process of starting and running a business with lots of useful practical advice to help you.

ISBN 978-1-84528-264-6

RUNNING A BED AND BREAKFAST: A LANDLADY'S GUIDE
CHRISTABEL MILNER

'Plenty of advice on the realities of running a B&B and its day-to-day management.' – *Best*

'The perfect escape plan.' – *Brand New You*

'Milner is like the sensible aunt you never had, full of amusing tales and common sense.' – *French Magazine*

'Anecdotal and easy to read, but full of detailed practical advice and the important lessons that need to be learnt. Covers everything from understanding the realities of running a B&B to its day to day management.' – *Food and Catering*

'An absolute gem of a book, which I enjoyed reading very much. Very clear and precise as well as entertaining.' – *The Landlord Law Blog*

ISBN 978-1-84528-269-1

MASTERING BOOK-KEEPING
DR PETER MARSHALL
An accredited textbook of The Institute of Chartered Bookkeepers.

This updated 8th edition contains extracts from ICB, AAT, OCR and AQA sample examination papers.

'This book has been planned to cover the requirements of all the major examining boards' syllabuses and achieves all it sets out to do.' – *Focus on Business Education*

'Presented in a clear and logical manner – written in plain English.' – *Learning Resources News*

'This book has great potential value.' – *Educational Equipment Magazine*

ISBN 978-1-84528-324-7

Swindon Libraries
01793 707120
Thank you for using
North Swindon Library

Borrowed Items 28/11/2009
XXXXX65006

Item Details	Due Date
Proper care and feeding o	19/12/200
Start and run a shop :	19/12/200

WRITING A WINNING BUSINESS PLAN
MATTHEW RECORD

'This book will not only help you prepare a business plan but will also provide a basic understanding of how to start up a business.' – *Working from Home*

'An excellent reference for even the most inexperienced business person looking to march into the business world ably armed with a professional plan.' – *Home Business Alliance*

ISBN 978-1-84528-302-5

THE SMALL BUSINESS START-UP WORKBOOK
CHERYL D. RICKMAN

'I would urge every business adviser in the land to read this book' – *Sylvia Tidy-Harris, Managing Director of www.womenspeakers.co.uk*

'Inspirational and practical workbook that takes you from having a business idea to actually having a business. By the time you have worked through the exercises and checklists you will be focused, confident and raring to go.'
– *www.allthatwomenwant.co.uk*

'A real "must have" for anyone thinking of setting up their own venture.' – *Thames Valley News*

'… a very comprehensive book, a very readable book.' – *Sister Business E-Zine*

ISBN 978-1-84528-038-3

SETTING UP & RUNNING A LIMITED COMPANY
ROBERT BROWNING

'Many businesses are run though companies but there are legal implications, and careful consideration required before forming a limited company. This guide sets out the pros and cons, and how to proceed.' – *Landlordzone.co.uk*

ISBN 978-1-85703-866-8

HOW TO GET FREE PUBLICITY
PAM AND BOB AUSTIN

This step-by-step manual is ideal for small businesses, clubs, schools or charities. In it you'll discover how to present stories that will get accepted by editors and how to write effective press releases and articles and deal with media interviews.

ISBN 978-1-84528-180-9

85 INSPIRING WAYS TO MARKET YOUR SMALL BUSINESS
JACKIE JARVIS

This book sets out some great ideas and explains how each idea will benefit your business, what you need to do to make it work, and how you can apply it to your own business *immediately*.

ISBN 978-1-84528-396-4

How To Books are available through all good bookshops, or you can order direct from us through Grantham Book Services.

Tel: +44 (0)1476 541080
Fax: +44 (0)1476 541061
Email: **orders@gbs.tbs-ltd.co.uk**

Or via our website

www.howtobooks.co.uk

To order via any of these methods please quote the title(s) of the book(s) and your credit card number together with its expiry date.

For further information about our books and catalogue, please contact:

How To Books
Spring Hill House,
Spring Hill Road,
Begbroke
Oxford OX5 1RX,

Visit our web site at **www.howtobooks.co.uk**

Or you can contact us by email at **info@howtobooks.co.uk**